Belvoir

Archaeologies of Restorative Justice

Series Editors

Edward González-Tennant

Ben Ford

BELVOIR

AN ARCHAEOLOGY OF MARYLAND SLAVERY

JULIE M. SCHABLITSKY

THE UNIVERSITY OF ALABAMA PRESS
TUSCALOOSA

PUBLISHED IN COOPERATION WITH THE
SOCIETY FOR HISTORICAL ARCHAEOLOGY

The University of Alabama Press
Tuscaloosa, Alabama 35487-0380
uapress.ua.edu

Typeface: Minion Pro

Cover images: *Above*, architectural 3-D model reconstruction of the Belvoir Quarter; *below*, buttons and transfer print ceramics; *back*, descendants standing on the footprint of Belvoir Quarter; courtesy of the Maryland Department of Transportation
Cover design: Sandy Turner Jr.

SOCIETY *for* HISTORICAL ARCHAEOLOGY

Cataloging-in-Publication data is available from the Library of Congress.
ISBN: 978-0-8173-2250-2 (cloth)
ISBN: 978-0-8173-6222-5 (paper)
E ISBN: 978 0 8173 9579 7

To the Brogden and Burley families,

Contents

Illustrations

Figures

Tables

Foreword

We are pleased to welcome you to the second book in the Archaeologies of Restorative Justice series copublished by the Society for Historical Archaeology and the University of Alabama Press. This series provides a forum for those who draw on historical archaeology's unique approach to unearth and share the histories of African, Asian, Indigenous, Pacific Islander, and other communities in settler societies like the United States. Building on years of research, activism, and community engagement, the Society for Historical Archaeology declared itself an antiracist organization in 2015. This initiative emerged from a broader effort to confront racism within the organization and the workplaces of its members. Led by the Gender and Minority Affairs Committee, this work began with antiracism training for the society's board, later expanding to the general membership. Recent efforts and statements by the society's board remind us that a commitment to diversity, equity, inclusivity, belonging, and mattering (DEIBM) initiatives is central to 21st-century historical archaeology.

We began this series after recognizing that collaboration is a core value of many archaeological projects foregrounding social justice. The centering of community concerns at each stage of these projects opens spaces for communities and individuals to engage with historical archaeologists as we cocreate projects that explore historical wrongs. This guides the construction of expanded narratives, which in turn provide new material for expanding public conversations and contributing to positive social change.

Although the term *restorative justice* may be unfamiliar to historical archaeologists, many of its tenets are not. Restorative justice foregrounds healing and calls on perpetrator groups to acknowledge their wrongdoing as a part of working toward reconciliation. Many archaeologists, trained in programs dominated by Anglo-American, upper-class, male, and hetero individuals, are more familiar with retributive justice and its focus on punishment. This fixation on defining supposedly appropriate punishments for breaking the law produces a distorted view of reality, contributing to monstrous disparities. Historically, in the United States and elsewhere, this often results in minority communities experiencing higher rates of policing with greater numbers of individuals from these groups incarcerated for relatively mild crimes (e.g., possession of cannabis). While legal scholars increasingly adopt the language of restorative justice, we find its clearest expression among Indigenous justice systems.

Keeping this in mind, we are proud to welcome Julie Schablitsky as an author in the Archaeologies of Restorative Justice series. Schablitsky's work bridges the academic and professional realms of historical archaeology as evidenced by a robust publication record while serving as the head of Cultural Resources for the Maryland Department of Transportation. *Belvoir: An Archaeology of Maryland Slavery* touches upon many of the central tenets of restorative justice. Collaboration remains central to understanding the importance of Belvoir in the present, unlocking the true potential of the project. As Schablitsky repeatedly notes, including descendant voices is crucial when exploring historical sites associated with slavery, where trauma and oppression have left indelible marks on the collective psyche.

Schablitsky effortlessly weaves contemporary theory into her analysis and presents a living history of Belvoir. In doing so, she offers a corrective to persistent myths regarding the lives of enslaved Africans and their descendants in the United States. Belvoir Quarter is rendered as a rich homeplace, its kitchen's ceramic assemblage speaks to defying European customs, and slate pencils and tablets attest to educational aspirations of Belvoir's residents. In the compelling case of Belvoir, archaeology reveals how the daily lives of enslaved persons rejected the totalizing attempts to define them by the site's enslavers. Schablitsky's book contributes to restorative justice by crafting a historical narrative that resonates with descendants and provides insights for the public regarding the struggles and sacrifice of the site's enslaved residents.

The Archaeologies of Restorative Justice series similarly highlights the deep connections between the past and present. Historical archaeology offers a powerful tool for crafting historical narratives erased through structural and symbolic means. We see that engaging a state's Department of Transportation, which often threatens to destroy minority communities and/or their material remains across the nation, in this sort of work is a powerful reminder of the role applied archaeologists can play in supporting positive social change.

Archaeologies of Restorative Justice provides an outlet for archaeologists who bend our discipline toward positive social change. It is promoted to the entire Society for Historical Archaeology and broader global audience through the combined society and University of Alabama Press networks. Royalties from this series are directed to the society's antiracism fund. This supports our entire community as we continue our work against racism, sexism, and injustice within and throughout historical archaeology. Expanding the circle of support for restorative justice within the Society for Historical

Archaeology, the society and members Thomas Layton and David Hurst Thomas have dedicated funds for Archaeologies of Restorative Justice writing stipends. These funds will bring new and underrepresented voices into the discussion of restorative justice in archaeology. As you read this and other titles in our series, consider how you might join the conversation and realize archaeology's unique potential for building a better future.

Edward González-Tennant
Edinburg, Texas

Ben Ford
Indiana, Pennsylvania

Acknowledgments

I AM THANKFUL to the Maryland Department of Transportation (MDOT) for supporting archaeology stewardship projects along our highways. This agency appreciates the value of discovering and sharing Maryland history with the public. These projects have profound and positive impacts on descendant communities, tourism, and interagency relationships. I am grateful to the former MDOT State Highway Administration leadership team including Neil Pedersen, Doug Simmons, Raja Veeramachaneni, Bruce Grey, Don Sparklin, and Greg Slater for their trust and unwavering support for Maryland history and cultural resources.

The archaeological discovery of the Belvoir Quarter would not have been possible without the encouragement of former property owners, Rockbridge Academy, including Angela and Nate Bailey. Anne Arundel County archaeologists Jane Cox, Al Luckenbach (retired), Shawn Sharp, and other county staff assisted on this project as we moved through the discovery process. Aaron Levinthal was invaluable on site and assisted me in directing the project. Consultant firms and individuals providing technical expertise included New South Associates, AECOM, and Robert Selig. Ralph Koziarski served as the faunal analyst, and Kathy Furgerson analyzed the macrobotanical remains. The artifact analysis was carried out by Adam Fracchia, Alex Keim, Jerry Warner, and Aaron Levinthal with final curatorial preparation and artifact photographs by Sarah Janesko. The site location maps were created by Andrew Bernish while Sean Jones is acknowledged for formatting the figures. Dennis Pogue and Doug Sanford visited the site to provide insight, while Pogue further assisted in the virtual reconstruction of the Belvoir Quarter. Terry Kilby and Direct Dimensions scanned the site and captured drone images of the landscape providing new and unique perspectives on the site. Heather Roche and her canines surveyed the cemetery helping us confirm its discovery.

I deeply appreciate the support of the surrounding neighborhood, local elected officials, and descendant community. The late Thomas Carroll Worthington openly shared his home and family history with us. It was an honor to meet him. I recognize and thank Janice Hayes-Williams who brought attention and excitement from Annapolis to Belvoir. She connected me with the descendants. I am grateful for the Burley and Brogden descendants, including Nancy Daniels, Shelley Evans, Erica Jones, Wanda Watts, Pamela Brogden, Sheila Brogden-Jefferson, Vernon Brogden, and others, who participated in the discovery of their family history. Their reverence for their ancestors gave meaning and value to this archaeological discovery.

Introduction

Digging and Discovering

NEAR ANNAPOLIS IN Anne Arundel County, Maryland, the historic site of Belvoir is hidden behind a thick stand of trees lining General's Highway (Figure I.1). Named for George Washington, this now-paved colonial road connects Baltimore and Annapolis. Between the 18th and 19th centuries, the 6,000-acre tobacco plantation boasted an impressive landscape of brick and stone homes and buildings. At least 30 enslaved people at one time worked in Belvoir's fields, gardens, and buildings. Today, the estate has dwindled to 144 acres and is encroached upon by an upscale housing subdivision (Figure I.2). Although the colonial outbuildings are gone, the manor house still stands adjacent to an eroded terraced garden filled with aged boxwoods and cherry trees. Few people know the historic site exists. Over the last decade, the property has passed from one nonprofit to another, with no clear preservation plan in place. Belvoir's potential to interpret the lives of many families and people lies untapped, and its future remains unknown.

In 1967, the Maryland Department of Transportation (MDOT) marked this site with a cast-metal roadside historical marker as the spot where French commander Le Comte Rochambeau and his men camped on August 17, 1781, before making their way to Yorktown. MDOT supports a public archaeology stewardship program that researches historic sites along highways with a connection to transportation. These initiatives include partnerships with public agencies and descendant communities. As an archaeologist, I was intrigued by Belvoir's link to the American Revolution and decided to locate the French commander's camp to further interpret this history along our highway. I wanted to know where Rochambeau camped with his men and find what they left behind. A team of one dozen archaeologists searched the estate, one hole at a time. After excavating across acres of land and waving metal detectors across Belvoir's grassy fields, we never found evidence of a Revolutionary War–era campsite. The French commander, his men, and

Figure I.1. Map with Belvoir, Annapolis, General's Highway, and Severn River. (Base map from Esri. Map by Andrew Bernish, Courtesy of the Maryland Department of Transportation.)

Figure I.2. Bird's-eye view of Belvoir oriented north with the stone and brick manor home in the lower right and the quarter location under the small white building on far-right center of image. The subdivision is located to the south and east of the buildings. (Courtesy of the Maryland Department of Transportation.)

camp followers were gone; they left no trace. Before Rochambeau slept here, Francis Scott Key's great-grandparents built a tobacco plantation with a stone manor house and homes for the enslaved people. As fate would have it, instead of finding France, we found Africa.

In colonial Maryland, the economy was deeply rooted in a slave society, a system upheld by the aristocratic families who settled here. Already entitled and accustomed to being served and benefited by others' sacrifice, slavery was palatable to those who needed massive amounts of cheap labor to grow the young country. When I studied newspaper advertisements about enslaved people, the wills of wealthy planters, and family letters, the inhumanity and complexities of bound servitude were shocking and complicated. While unsurprising, these human traffickers held contradictory and ugly racist ideologies and subjected their enslaved people to a brutal and inhumane existence. Today, we view the notion of a slave system as pure insanity, and studying the musings and letters of enslavers is horrifying. Sometimes their writings appear wicked yet oddly paternalistic, while other enslavers are brutally honest and hateful toward human chattel. The responses from enslaved people attempting to survive these circumstances varied; some resisted bondage by withholding labor and self-emancipating, while others simply tried to exist through submissive behavior appearing as Stockholm syndrome. In the end, the experiment of using enslaved labor to grow the colonies and make America great was the epitome of human greed and evil. But how does the public react to these painful truths, and how do educators respond to this shameful past?

Teaching difficult history is uncomfortable. Many educators appreciate the importance of sharing the dark past in a classroom setting, but they struggle with the delivery. Publications on slavery are often limited in scope and depth, and subsequently, Black history fails to be properly incorporated into American history. A recent example included a third-grade class in Annapolis. Reading the children's book *Henry's Freedom Box* (Levine 2007) is a popular and a safe way to introduce elementary-aged students to slavery. At an almost exclusively white attended private elementary school in Annapolis, the educator had my child draw and label his own "runaway slave ad" for Henry. The teaching of Black history with traumatic elements using apathetic lessons and untrained educators causes more harm than *not* teaching it. I sent an email to the educator at the school, attempting to use this miserable assignment as a teachable moment, and attached historic "runaway ads" to underscore the problem. I received no reply. Our education system, however, is not the only institution failing at delivering an antiracist history.

The average American learns about Black history by visiting historic plantations across the southeastern United States. Usually, these sites celebrate the economic and political achievements of white men as countless visitors pass through the elaborate halls of their home and stroll across manicured lawns and ornamental gardens. Over the last decade, tours focused on the lives of enslaved people have increased at the homes of dead American presidents and others. The interpretation of cabins for enslaved families is simple and consistent between dwellings, with corn husk filled mattresses on the floor, gourd dippers hung on the wall, and wooden bowls sitting on crudely made wooden furniture. Unfortunately, docents may even romanticize the lives of enslaved people by sharing stories of love and friendship between "master and slave," while others may shock visitors with morbid tales of shackles anchored into basement walls and floors. While I appreciate the limitations of some historic house museums, the history of slavery should never be idealized, justified, or sensationalized: basements were kitchens and not a place to shackle people, and "love" between the captive and captor was rape.

THE DISCOVERY

The objective of this book is not to judge Maryland's planter families or the apathetic misinterpretations of the past by the present, but to reright by rewriting at least one story from the Chesapeake region using Belvoir as the stage. It is important to demonstrate the varied lived experiences of enslaved people using scientific evidence supported by the written record. As such, our mission as archaeologists is to discover information about our buried past that cannot be located anywhere else; when the historical record is silent, archaeology can be noisy. Admittedly, not all archaeological sites are valuable; sometimes artifacts cannot tell us much at all, or what they tell us can just as easily be found in historical records. But we must always shake the soil and ask each historic place what is left to learn. Through the study of material culture or artifacts and structural remains, we have an opportunity with Belvoir to understand how enslaved people kept their humanity and persevered despite living within an oppressive and abusive society.

Today, Belvoir includes a ca. 1736 home along with later additions, an early 20th-century barn, and a mid-20th-century tenant house. The surrounding land to the east and south, once part of the larger Belvoir estate, is now a subdivision. Since our metal detecting surveys and excavations across the yards failed to turn up artifacts from the 1781 Rochambeau occupation, I suspect evidence of the camp was destroyed by modern development. It is also possible the property at Belvoir was so heavily tilled, grazed, and eroded that any ephemeral evidence, such as temporary ovens, lead shot, and buttons, dissipated long ago making the site unlikely to be found by our survey methods.

We also searched downslope from the manor house and placed 1-1/2ft.-diameter shovel test pits every 15 ft. on a grid pattern and pushed soil through our sieves to catch artifacts. Near an extant but abandoned, later 20th-century tenant house located downhill from the manor house, we recovered larger and older 18th-century ceramic sherds in one of the holes. The high number and type of artifacts suggested an older and buried home site separate from the manor home. Next, we placed a 5 ft. × 5 ft. excavation unit between the hole and the tenant house. Here, we found large, tumbled rocks with more artifacts. I then directed the excavation of a second unit in front of the tenant house. Over a foot down, there was an intact, 2-ft.-wide mortared stone building foundation. Dirt square after dirt square, we followed the stone foundation wall to each corner. We realized the later 20th-century tenant house was placed on top of ca. 1900 concrete foundation, which was then placed on top of an even earlier stone foundation (Figure I.3). We stretched our long tape from corner to corner and measured the stone foundation. We had delineated a 32-ft. square, stone building.

Figure I.3. View of tenant house on top of Belvoir Quarter. The southwest corner of stone foundation in foreground with brick interior flooring in center with brick interior wall to left. (Courtesy of the Maryland Department of Transportation.)

As we excavated the exterior and the interior of this building, I kept wondering who lived in this stone house with a brick floor. The earliest ceramic sherds dated to around the 1780s, just after the American Revolution. Dr. Upton Scott and his wife, Elizabeth Ross, lived here during that time. I knew from historical records the Ireland-born doctor had been temporarily banished from Annapolis and accused of being a Tory. Perhaps he focused his attention and money on improving his estate during that time. Initially, I believed the home was too well built for enslaved people, and the appearance of brass waistcoat buttons and broken teacups confused me further. I reviewed the 1798 tax record that listed all improvements on the property. It revealed Henry Maynadier, Scott's nephew, managed the estate at the time and one of the buildings he was taxed for was a 32 ft. × 32 ft. "stone negro quarter." There was no doubt this is what we found; it was the right date, right location, and right size. The artifacts dated through the mid-19th century, confirming the home was lived in by enslaved people until Maryland's emancipation on November 1, 1864. The doorways and windows within the stone walls kept their shape as they bloomed open and wilted in place, inadvertently protecting artifacts previously tossed out the windows and doors. The Belvoir Quarter was a time capsule that held architectural features in place with layers of artifacts spanning more than over 80 years.

ORGANIZATION OF THE BOOK

This book takes the discovery of a stone quarter built for enslaved people, along with its material culture, and discusses the finds in the context of other similar sites of enslavement. Each broken sherd, tobacco pipestem, and button contributes to our understanding of how enslaved people existed and resisted. My interpretation of the artifacts and archaeology demonstrate that, despite being enslaved, this community was not simply reactionary or stagnant within their environment due to their situation. Instead, these enslaved people consciously and purposefully reacted within and forged their own identities and realities (Dornan 2002).

The first chapter focuses on the reason behind publishing a publicly accessible archaeology story: the descendant community. Civic engagement in archaeology is an approach touted as a "best practice" in applied anthropology programs, particularly by those working with African American descendants. Here, I share the impact an inclusive archaeology project can have on an entire community. While archaeology allowed the Burley and Brogden families to find their roots and see the objects left behind, the stories connected to the site told of sacrifice and tragic loss.

Chapter 2 relies on the archival record to reconstruct the history of the planter families. Documents of people who lived their lives enslaved at Belvoir are limited to the enslavers' wills and a few self-liberation ads; however, I use these to say their names and demonstrate the bravery it took to resist, overcome, and survive. After studying the enslaver families' correspondence between one another, I was reminded about the emotional and mental complexities of human beings and the power of compartmentalization. Reading about their emotional pain from losing a child, health issues, and detecting frustration in the tone of handwritten letters while they navigated life in a colonial world humanizes the enslavers in some ways. I detected love and commitment to family but also evil and hate toward others. The Rosses, Scotts, Worthingtons, and Welshes believed freedom was their birthright and enslavement was the Africans' destiny. Truly, they are on the wrong side of history. During an oral history interview, I asked Thomas Worthington, descendent of Brice John Worthington, his thoughts about being descended from ancestors who enslaved people. Mr. Worthington's tone became serious, and he recalled what his father told him, "If we knew some of our family members today, we wouldn't even allow them on our land" (Worthington 2015). Indeed, the sins of their forefathers are not theirs. While the historical context and position of the planter families may stir emotions within us, their position and perspective should instead be used in this context as a backdrop for the archaeology of the Africans and African Americans who labored and persevered at Belvoir. It tells us who they lived among and resisted against.

The third chapter provides a detailed discussion of what we know about the homes of enslaved people from archaeological sites, enslavers' written descriptions, and architectural drawings. Although the types of homes in the Chesapeake region differed based on availability of materials and wealth of the estate, they seldom built the homes to last. I used what is known about the living quarters of enslaved people to explore our discovery of the Belvoir Quarter with its unique footprint and stone construction. This home also supported a subfloor pit that was used over the years by two different enslaved communities, making it possible to compare their diets over time. Since the flooring, foundation, and fireplaces survived enough to be virtually reconstructed, we followed the archaeological findings to resurrect the building to provide a snapshot in time.

Chapters 4 through 6 use the material culture left within and immediately around the Belvoir Quarter to understand the enslaved people who lived there between the 1780s and 1864. First, a detailed discussion ensues covering the variety of ceramics, decorative techniques, and forms used to prepare and serve meals from the kitchen. Here, I consider how enslaved people acquired and chose the various dishwares based on vessel form and decoration allowing their agency to materialize. The chapter following this discussion focuses on the faunal remains (animal bones) related to their meals. While the data of wild and domestic animal species are displayed in graphs, I also consider differences among Belvoir's enslaved communities and compare these findings with other similar archaeological sites.

Chapter 6 reveals how enslaved people clothed themselves with a detailed analysis of the types of buttons used to fasten some of the formal pieces like overcoats and waistcoats. Since these fasteners are common on archaeological sites, some scholars have considered alternative functions of buttons as ways enslaved people signaled affluence and relevance to each other. Belvoir's large copper alloy button assemblage allowed analysis and my consideration of the enslaved community using these fasteners. Their lost beads and jewelry also provided a chance to consider their individual style. Following this discussion, I consider the power of the tobacco pipe not only as a way to publicly communicate personal interests and beliefs but as a way to connect enslaved people back to Africa using DNA.

The final chapter uses artifacts related to guns and knives, spiritual beliefs, and writing to reflect on the various reasons and ways enslaved people at Belvoir may have pushed back against their situation. Admittedly, it is uncommon to find archaeological evidence of rebellions, so we turn to everyday items including dropped slate pencils, hidden knives, and buried animal bones to detect subtle acts of resistance. I conclude by circling back to Belvoir's descendants and sharing the various perspectives gleaned from them while they experienced the history of their ancestors through written records and artifacts. In the end, they reminded us how invaluable community and the sacredness of space can be after uncovering difficult history.

The archaeological study of the Belvoir Quarter provides us with a well-preserved stone quarter to exhibit everyday material culture, to consider enslaved people's agency, and to illuminate the human will it took to preserve their humanity in a homeplace. The artifact assemblage is spectacular, and the thousands of items allowed us to witness the prosaic moments of life within the home, yet consider how and why they chose particular patterns, colors, and images on ceramic dishwares and tobacco pipes. A handful of descriptions from self-liberation newspaper ads and historical descriptions provide an opportunity to envision the uniforms various enslaved people wore and how buttons and beads may have been used to signal a person's awareness to style and status. I use the robust archival record of the Scotts and the Worthingtons to expose their hypervigilance with maintaining wealth and their apathy regarding the morality of using human chattel to achieve it. From all of this, I hope the reader comes away with a better understanding of Maryland history and recognizes how African diaspora archaeology is a method to find and learn about the strength of people who were placed in a system that attempted to strip them of their culture and identity. Despite the trauma and oppression, they persevered and continue to survive in their living descendants.

Furthermore, while the consultation and inclusion of descendants should be the cornerstone of all archaeological projects, it is especially important for historic sites like Belvoir where slavery and human brutality took place. Descendants often have little written history of their family, and knowing their ancestors endured a life of poverty and periods of torture can be a burden. Bearing witness to the production of knowledge and the discovery of artifacts once held in their family's hands can be therapeutic and healing. Archaeology is the production of data through artifact and site analysis, but it is most importantly a vehicle to reunite living communities with their past.

Belvoir

1
Descending and Honoring

> When I was a little girl, my grandmother would tell me our family history while riding the train. She said we came from Anne Arundel, down in the country. I never knew where she meant, until now. It was here she was talking about, Belvoir.
>
> —Nancy Daniels, Burley descendant

African diaspora sites hold unique and often traumatic stories about our past. When these types of sites are investigated, we need descendants to help direct and inform our research path. As an archaeologist, I have the knowledge and methods to find, excavate, and interpret historic sites, but my ancestry and lived experiences prevent me from knowing and fully comprehending the impact of racism and oppression on someone of African descent. The emotional and mental impression from the discovery of a quarter for enslaved people will land differently with me than someone descended from an enslaved person. The meaning of homeplace as a sanctuary and refuge from intimidation and racial violence, for example, is different for Black people than white people (Hooks 2015:41). This concept alone demonstrates the challenge I faced before even beginning to understand the Belvoir Quarter. Despite these limitations, there is support and direction from my Black colleagues and descendant communities. Their guidance is crucial and necessary for me to navigate successfully through projects with African American history. I must also be actively and continually learning, monitoring, and self-correcting in my scholarship and personal life. As archaeologists, we are responsible for sharing knowledge about historic sites with these descendants, answering hard questions, and, most importantly, listening to what they want to know. Over numerous visits, emails, and phone calls, I formed close relationships with the families. I was humbled by their trust and understood my role as *their* archaeologist.

Janice Hayes-Williams, a passionate Annapolis historian, quickly knew the importance of Belvoir's discovery to Maryland history. She contacted Larry Brogden, whose surname is associated with the site, and he shared the news with Vernon Brogden. Then, Hayes-Williams reached out to Nancy Daniels, who was the four-time great-granddaughter of Anne Burley, enslaved by the Worthington family, who lived on the adjacent estate. Daniels is a skilled genealogist who knew the ancestors' names but not the location of their homes. The Worthingtons purchased Belvoir after Scott. There were other family members in the community too. Shelley Evans, also a four-time great-granddaughter of the Burleys, contacted Daniels after finding connections in their family tree. They were told about the archaeological discovery. Evans brought her sister, Wanda Watts, and daughter, Erica Jones, with her to visit Belvoir. Brogden shared the story with his daughters: Verna Brogden, Pamela Brogden, Sheila Brogden-Jefferson, Glenda Brogden-Ballentine, Lisa Brogden-Mellerson, and Tonya Brogden. They could all trace their ancestors to the Worthington family, who once owned Belvoir and the adjacent estate. They visited Belvoir, attended archaeology presentations, and learned about the place where their relatives likely lived and worked. Through the descendants' words and their silence, there was sadness imagining what their ancestors endured to give them life, yet a feeling of excitement in connecting with what had been lost and now found. Daniels was openly emotional about visiting the location her family knew; the experience was "unbelievable awe, a feeling that could not be described with words" (WBAL-11 2020). Many genealogists can appreciate the excitement of finding a family name handwritten in an old document. The opportunity to walk in the footsteps of ancestors is rarely felt by descendants. Daniels's sleuthing gave her family a gift, and the discovery of Belvoir felt like acknowledgment from above. One day at the site, she pulled out an empty pill bottle from her pocket and scraped it across the ground, filling the amber-colored container full of the sacred soil. After the dig, each descendant carried home an old handmade brick from the archaeologists' discard pile. I wonder about the stories they tell about the brick, mentioning how it was once part of the home where their ancestors lived at Belvoir.

The others, including Watts, felt intense emotions when Belvoir could be linked to Africa (Schablitsky et al. 2019a). It gave her a connection to the past she never felt before (WBAL-11 2020). There was a renewed sense of pride and excitement she shared on phone calls and across social media sites tagging her family. Jones, the five-time great-granddaughter of Thomas and Anne Burley, found the entire experience emotional and humbling. Brice John Worthington enslaved dozens of people throughout his lifetime, including Anne and her daughter, Ellen. He owned a beautiful home in the center of Annapolis but primarily lived on a large estate adjacent to Belvoir (*Maryland Gazette* [*MG*] 1816). When Belvoir went on the market in 1815, he waited, and then purchased it right before auction. Worthington owned it until his death in 1837. Between this time, Thomas Burley bought the freedom of his wife, Anne, and daughter, Ellen. He memorialized the manumission in 1854, stating, "Whereas many years since I purchased from a certain Brice J. Worthington Esquire my wife a coloured woman by the name of Anne and daughter Ellen being at the time slaves for life" (Burley Manumission 1854:86). There is no mention of which estate the Burley women lived and worked on in Anne Arundel County, but it was either Belvoir or the adjacent Worthington estate. If the Burleys did not reside at Belvoir, they lived next door, and it was likely their family labored on both estates. We know from Daniels's genealogy work and DNA testing that she is related to the Brogdens, whose ancestors may have lived at Belvoir in the stone quarter. Additionally, the 1840 U.S. Federal Census enumerated Abraham Brogden in Anne Arundel County living adjacent to the families of Solomon Brogden and Nicholas Burley. They were part of the same community.

Worthington's 1837 will only mentioned an enslaved community living at Belvoir, suggesting he either sold or transferred ownership of them before his death. Those living at Belvoir included Cinderella, who was married by 1848 to a freed man, Abraham Brogden. Brogden was a farm laborer who lived in Baltimore City but worked on James Curley's farm. He had a reputation in his community, among both white and Black citizens, of being "honest, sober, and industrious" as did his father and grandfather (Anne Arundel County Pardon Record 1851). At some point, George Worthington, Belvoir's heir, was in debt and considered selling the woman he enslaved, Cinderella (Anne Arundel County Pardon Record 1851). The reason he chose her is unknown; perhaps she had a history of resisting, fighting her entrapment through elopement and work refusal. Discussions of the imminent sale of Cinderella reached the African American community, including her husband. The sale of people, particularly to the Deep South, was a cruel maneuver that separated families and resulted in harsher work conditions. Brogden refused to allow his wife to be sold across state lines. Unable to buy her freedom, they made the decision for Cinderella to self-emancipate. On December 21, 1848, Cinderella gathered up her clothing and left Belvoir with her husband.

Immediately, Worthington's overseer, Edward H. Brown, placed an ad for $100 for her return (*Baltimore Sun* [*BS*] 1848) (Figure 1.1). Before the ad hit the newspaper, they were caught in Baltimore. Brogden was incarcerated for "enticing a slave to runaway" (Anne Arundel County Pardon Record 1851). Incensed by Brogden's imprisonment, the white community of Annapolis attempted to free him through the governor's pardon. Letters were written in support of Brogden and his family's good character, and an explanation of the situation was reported to the county. The letters pointed out the stark contrast between supporting a husband attempting to keep his wife from being sold to pay off a debt and the agenda of the "fanatic and political abolitionists" who wanted to eliminate slavery altogether (Anne Arundel County Pardon Record 1851). The response by the white community to the incarceration of Brogden is curious and was unlikely inspired by altruism but rather by Curley's reliance on Brogden for the success of his farm or perhaps from a serious plea made by Brogden's family to a white ally. After serving three years of the four-year term, Brogden was pardoned on May 23, 1851, by Governor Lowe. The letter to Governor Lowe mentioned Cinderella was sold outside of Maryland and died (Anne Arundel County Pardon Record 1851). They believed sharing these details demonstrated the impossible likelihood of Brogden reoffending. Unfortunately, we do not know where Cinderella died or where she is buried.

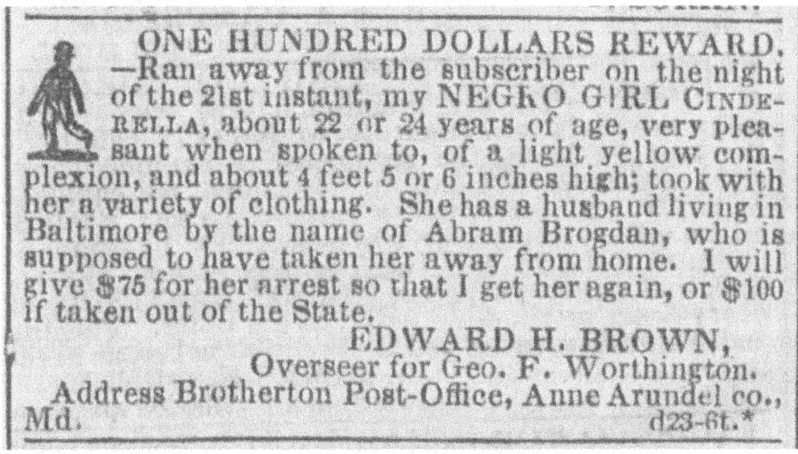

ONE HUNDRED DOLLARS REWARD.—Ran away from the subscriber on the night of the 21st instant, my NEGRO GIRL CINDERELLA, about 22 or 24 years of age, very pleasant when spoken to, of a light yellow complexion, and about 4 feet 5 or 6 inches high; took with her a variety of clothing. She has a husband living in Baltimore by the name of Abram Brogdan, who is supposed to have taken her away from home. I will give $75 for her arrest so that I get her again, or $100 if taken out of the State.

EDWARD H. BROWN,
Overseer for Geo. F. Worthington.
Address Brotherton Post-Office, Anne Arundel co., Md. d23-6t.*

Figure 1.1. Newspaper advertisement of Cinderella Brogden self-liberating with the help of her husband, Abraham Brogden. (Courtesy of the Maryland State Archives.)

Although Cinderella's life ended, Brogden was able to successfully rebuild his life and eventually remarried. In the 1870 U.S. Federal Census, he was 50 years old and living in Philadelphia with his 33-year-old second wife, Margaret. They had five children (Jerusha [17], Sarah E. [16], Rowena [9], Georgiana [4], and James [1]) with the first child, Jerusha, born around 1853, two years after Abraham was pardoned. By 1880, the Brogden family added a daughter, Rachel, to the family. By then, Brogden worked as a meat smoker and lived with his wife and younger children in Philadelphia. His daughter Rowena Sharp also lived with him, while her husband, Moses L. Sharp, was incarcerated at the Pennsylvania state prison for an unknown offense (U.S. Federal Census 1880). Abraham and Margaret's living descendants include Pamela Brogden, Sheila Jefferson-Brogden, Vernon Brogden, and their families. Interestingly, Eliza Brogden, Cinderella's sister who lived with George

Figure 1.2. Meeting with descendants, archaeologists, and community members at the manor home at Belvoir. Here, archaeologists shared preliminary findings while answering questions and listening to input from descendants and community members. Seated around the table are: Lyndra Marshall (née Pratt), Barabara Paca, and Erica Jones (*left, bottom to top*), Wanda Watts (*center*), Janice Hayes-Williams, Theodore Mack, and Nancy Daniels (*right, top to bottom*). (Courtesy of the Maryland Department of Transportation.)

Worthington before she self-emancipated, also shared the same last name. Either the sisters' maiden name was Brogden, or they both married Brogden men. This is where the written record for the descendants' enslaved ancestors stopped, and their journey into archaeology began.

The Brogden and Burley descendants reached Belvoir by turning at the black-and-white cast-iron sign announcing Rochambeau's camp. Hitting the dirt road, they drove through a small stand of deciduous trees that opened to a rolling bucolic grassy field. Historically, it may have been planted in crops or used to graze animals. The rutted road carried them uphill past a small modern house on the left before they took a hairpin turn to the right placing them atop a hill next to a massive brick house, the home of their ancestors' enslaver. Watts felt two strong and very different emotions at once.

She was excited to know her family had lived here, only 22 miles away from her. Watts drove past Belvoir dozens of times on her way to the Maryland Black Caucus meetings, never knowing her connection to the place. She also felt sadness and pain, acutely aware of what happened there. The other descendants looked around without talking, posed for photos with their family, and walked with purpose along the brick walkway to the entrance. As we went to open the front door, the doorknob turned without unlatching, and the old wood door jamb stuck. It was as if the house did not want to let us in. But we were here and had work to do. The descendants entered the foyer, absorbing the experience, and turned right into the formal dining room. They and members of the Maryland Commission for African American History and Culture, Rockbridge Academy staff, and archaeologists found their seats. Watts deliberately placed herself at the head of the table (Figure 1.2).

2
Building and Enslaving

> My grandfather [Charles Worthington] had a voice that was left over from the slave days. He came out on the porch and said, "JOHN. I want to talk to you." John [who was formerly enslaved by Charles] answered, "Yes, Mr. Charlie." And then he [John] leaned over to me and said, "Little Tommy, a long time ago, I use to belong to your granddaddy and sometimes I think he still thinks I do."
>
> —Thomas Carroll Worthington Jr. (2015), Worthington descendant

Originally referred to as Beare Ridge, Belvoir was part of a large tract of land first patented in 1649 by Nicholas Wyatt from Virginia. Dying a wealthy landowner, Wyatt passed half of the property, including Belvoir, to his daughter, Sarah, and her husband, Colonel Edward Dorsey, in 1673 (Condon 2001; Selig 2015:9–10). The property stayed in the Dorsey family until Amos Garrett bought it in 1710, renaming it Providence. At the time of Garrett's death in 1727, the land was divided up and sold by his administrators. This estate has been home to numerous families over the years, but the Rosses, Scotts, Worthingtons, and Welshes were the planters and farmers who improved the property with enslaved labor. Although archaeology around the manor house was compromised from development and maintenance over the years, the archives contained government documents, letters, wills, and other primary sources. Dr. Upton Scott left a significant written record, while the others who came before and after him were only found in population and agricultural census records, wills, and a handful of family letters.

THE ROSS ESTATE

John Ross and his wife, Alicia Arnold, sailed to the Maryland colony from England in 1720 and 1723, respectively. Both the Ross and Arnold families were part of the aristocracy. Ross served as a colonial official for Lord Baltimore, while his wife claimed familial lineage from Charles Calvert, Fifth

Baron of Baltimore (Condon 2001:14–17; Selig 2015:10). Soon after settling in America, they had two daughters; Anne was born in 1727, and Elizabeth followed three years later. Around 1736, Ross purchased Providence and 733 acres. At the time, Belvoir was considered a "bare estate," perhaps located down by the Severn River, and only supported huts for enslaved and indentured servants, minimal animals, and farm equipment (Wetherill 1989:3). Ross's first major improvement was a stone house built from fieldstone on a prominent hill that overlooked the Severn River. Although it is incorporated into the main manor as a west wing today, Ross's original stone building was immediately adjacent to the road leading to Annapolis (Figure 2.1). Other buildings soon followed, including living quarters for enslaved people. By 1766, Ross enslaved over three dozen people (Ross 1766).

Figure 2.1. Stone house built by John Ross ca. 1736 on left and brick addition built by Dr. Scott during the 1780s. View toward northeast. (Courtesy of the Library of Congress, HABS MD, 2-CROWN.V. 1–2.)

Passing away after a stroke, Ross was remembered in Annapolis by the white press as a "tender Parent, indulgent Master, and kind Neighbour" (*MG* 1766). He willed Belvoir to his son-in-law, Dr. Scott, the spouse of his daughter Elizabeth, and divided up 37 enslaved people among his heirs. Ross gave his daughter Ann, who married Francis Key (Francis Scott Key's grandparents), the following enslaved people: four men, five women, seven boys, and two girls. Elizabeth received four men, three women, five girls, and four boys

(Selig 2015:11). One of the most brutal and feared outcomes of an enslaver's death was the separation of families. This played out the same at Belvoir. A quick study of Ross's will revealed many enslaved families but also many motherless children. The late Ned and Nan, for example, had three sons and two daughters, but by 1766, the parentless siblings were in jeopardy of being separated. As a result of Ross's death, one of the daughters stayed with Elizabeth Ross Scott while the other children were willed to Ann Ross Key and her three young children; Charles was given to John; Jem to Philip; and Bett was willed to Elizabeth (Ross 1766). Although ages are not provided in Ross's will, it is likely Nat's daughter, given to Elizabeth Ross Scott, was old enough to work in the house or field and, hence, separated from her family (Table 2.1).

Table 2.1. List of Enslaved People at Belvoir and Their Disposition, 1766.

Name	Sex	Age	Notes	New Enslaver
Phil	M	Adult		Ann Ross Key
Ned	M	Adult		Ann Ross Key
Ivory	M	Adult		Ann Ross Key
Tom	M	Adult		Ann Ross Key
Chloe	F	Adult		Ann Ross Key
Sylvia	F	Adult		Ann Ross Key
Kate	F	Adult		Ann Ross Key
Jerry	M	Child		Ann Ross Key
Bett	F	Adult		Ann Ross Key
Dick	M	Child		Ann Ross Key
Patt	F	Child		Ann Ross Key
Bob	M	Child		Ann Ross Key
Beck	F	Adult		Ann Ross Key
Charles	M	Child		Ann Ross Key
Tom	M	Child		Ann Ross Key
Tom	M	Child	Son of Pris (deceased)	Ann Ross Key
Lucy	F	Child	Daughter of Pris (deceased)	Ann Ross Key
Ned	M	Child	Son of Ned and Nan (deceased)	Ann Ross Key
Pompey	M	Adult		Elizabeth Ross Scott
Macey	M	Adult		Elizabeth Ross Scott
Dick	M	Adult		Elizabeth Ross Scott
Will	M	Adult		Elizabeth Ross Scott
Nell	F	Adult		Elizabeth Ross Scott
Kate	F			Elizabeth Ross Scott
Nan	F	Child	Mulatto	Elizabeth Ross Scott
Bill	M	Child	Mulatto	Elizabeth Ross Scott
Rose	F	Adult		Elizabeth Ross Scott
Pricilla	M	Child		Elizabeth Ross Scott
Rachell	F	Adult		Elizabeth Ross Scott
Mingo	M	Child		Elizabeth Ross Scott
Dick	M	Child	Mulatto/Son of Jenny (deceased)	Elizabeth Ross Scott

Name	Sex	Age	Notes	New Enslaver
Augustine	F	Child	Daughter of Jenny (deceased)	Elizabeth Ross Scott
Tammy	F	Child	Daughter of Jenny (deceased)	Elizabeth Ross Scott
Peg	F	Child	Daughter of Moll (deceased)	Elizabeth Ross Scott
Sal	F	Child	Daughter of Ned and Nan (deceased)	Elizabeth Ross Scott
Charles	M	Child	Son of Ned and Nan (deceased)	John Ross Key
Jem	M	Child	Son of Ned and Nan (deceased)	Philip Bardon Key
Bett	F	Child	Daughter of Ned and Nan (deceased)	Elizabeth Key

DR. UPTON SCOTT'S TENURE

Of Irish descent and educated in Scotland, Scott came to Annapolis in the fall of 1753 to serve as Maryland Governor Horatio Sharpe's personal physician (Selig 2015:17). Through this appointment he met many wealthy and politically connected Annapolitans, including John Ross's family. On September 5, 1756, Scott married Ross's daughter Elizabeth, who was described in the local newspaper as a "young Gentlewoman, with a pretty Fortune" (*MG* 1756). Anne, Elizabeth's sister, married Francis Key and moved away from Belvoir, while the Scotts were given an indenture from her father, John Ross, in 1758 that provided for their use of Belvoir during their natural lives (Provincial Court Land Records 1758).

Over the next decade, Scott actively acquired real estate and improved his landholdings. In 1762, he began constructing a stately brick house and outbuildings on 4 Shipwright Street in Annapolis; however, due to the unforeseen cost of construction, he went over budget and delayed completion of his home by almost three years (Seligman et al. 2006:28; Selig 2015:21). In a letter to his father, Scott wrote, "I am at present still exceedingly hampered on account of the expense of building a house which is not yet finished, my workman having pursued measures that have run away with more cash than I proposed" (Scott 1764). By the time the American Revolution was over, he was building again at Belvoir. After Scott inherited Belvoir from his father-in-law in 1766, he constructed a two-story brick addition onto the east wall of the stone house with a large front yard (Figure 2.2). Eventually, he added terraced gardens east and south of the manor. The view toward the Severn River from the front of the home would have been spectacular. Visitors arriving by water would have been greeted by a majestic view of the estate with the massive brick home accentuated by manicured plantings. During the last quarter of the 18th century, Scott constructed the stone quarter for enslaved people to the north and down the hill from his home. This building would have been physically separate but still within view and considered part of the manor complex. In addition to constructing expensive brick and stone buildings, he also designed and maintained formal gardens at both of his estates.

Figure 2.2. Brick addition built by Dr. Scott in the 1780s to overlook Round Bay and the Severn River. View toward west. (Courtesy of the Maryland Department of Transportation.)

THE FORMAL GARDENS

Serious thought went into the design and placement of the buildings, pastures, fields, and gardens on the landscape. This was the Age of Enlightenment, a period of rational thinking, reasoning, and science, and Scott likely embraced these principles among others. Manipulation of nature and artistic creativity within large gardens was done for aesthetics but also to accentuate the wealth and power of the planter. Scott attempted to communicate his influence within society through his knowledge of botany and the placement of terraced gardens on his property. He may have considered Belvoir, in comparison to his Annapolis home, as a large canvas where he could be creative and take calculated risks with the arrangement and use of space. Any diversions to his landscape plan would have been vetted among friends, and in the end, their opinions may have influenced the design and placement of buildings, features, and gardens. Scott was a member of the Tuesday Club of Annapolis, a place where discussions on science and philosophy were washed down with strong punch in the company of other elite Chesapeake men (Breslaw 1975). There was no shortage of opportunities to trade ideas and successful adaptations to one's property at these gatherings.

In addition to rolling hills and woods, Belvoir has a surviving formal terraced garden south of the manor house that once wrapped around to the front or east of the home. Unfortunately, the east terraces are all but erased by modern housing. Since this aspect served as the front of the house overlooking Round Bay and the Severn River, it would have been artfully sculpted and planted to greet visitors who arrived by boat. The southern yard has five extant terraces with a ramp in the middle. Although the garden still holds a variety of flowering trees and boxwoods, it would have historically supported vegetable plants, fruit trees, flowers, and a variety of shrubs. During its sale in 1816, Belvoir boasted an "extensive garden containing a choice collection of the best kinds of fruit, and the soil well suited to produce early vegetables; also, two extensive orchards of apples and peaches" (*MG* 1816).

The planter families used gardens as a space to spend leisure time and to share pride in botanical specimens with visitors. The number and variety of plantings required a head gardener and assistants under their direction to assist in planting, pruning, and harvesting these well-manicured terraces (Ball 1859:111–112). While visiting the estate in 1914, 100 years after the passing of Scott, John Martin Hammond (1914:223) marveled at this garden, writing, "The garden of Belvoir lies to the front of the house and even in its desolation to-day shows the beauty that must have been its own when in perfection. It has the outlook over Round Bay that is one of the great charms of the house and contains many shrubs and flowers which once on a time would have contented an observer near at hand, without his having to look to distance for beauty."

During the colonial period and through the early 19th century, opulence was communicated through possession and development of land. Homes were complementary to the larger estate and not necessarily the main or only symbol of wealth. Serious thought went into the garden and through this human design was born an expression of self and desire. Plantings of trees and installation of structures within the garden often created illusions of a larger home that visually accentuated the estate (Leone and Shackel 1990; Kryder-Reid 1998:273). Beautiful examples of these colonial gardens still survive in Annapolis at the William Paca House and Charles Carroll's home. Cultural landscape studies, particularly the study of terraced colonial gardens, have a place in archaeology. Examination of soils and botanical remains within these features can reveal the locations of beds and types of plantings. This evidence can be used to reconstruct some of the original plantings and prominent designs. When it comes to the formation of garden spaces and placement of botanical specimens, some scholars interpret a deeper meaning into the manipulation of landscape. Although we did not undertake explorations in garden archaeology, others have considered their arrangement. Leone (1988) interpreted formal gardens as a symbol of the planter communicating control over wealth and power. While this hypothesis may simplify the grand statement of manicuring nature, the importance of gardens to the colonial elite should not be understated.

Scott created Belvoir's gardens as landscape features to accentuate the estate's grandeur. It is also possible his fascination and intellect of various plants and herbs provided him with a sense of power over life. Knowledge of medicinal botany was necessary to effectively treat ailments. Through formal education, these healers gained knowledge about the human body and the effect of diseases upon them. Just as importantly, they learned which plants and herbs were helpful and harmful to humans. During the 18th and 19th centuries, physicians spent much of their time studying the power of plants, some even publishing books that helped the public determine which fruits, herbs, and beverages would help them heal sickness and stay healthy (Stearns 1801). A remedy for the bladder, for example, included the boiling of parsley roots and flaxseed into a beverage. Rheumatism, a chronic yet intermittent joint pain, would have been treated by drinking a hot tea made from burdock root and sassafras root bark (Worthington 1852–1856). They believed that "health was a natural state of the body which could be maintained and protected" (Risse 1992:149). These early medical practitioners recognized the power of nature and may have seen their gardens as places to grow and harness strength, ultimately influencing life and death.

Both a physician and tobacco planter, Scott was passionate about gardening for the challenge of collecting unique specimens from around the world but also for the healing power of herbs. While visiting Belvoir, David Warden (1811:132) noted that Scott was "fond of Botany, and has a number of rare plants and shrubs in his green house and garden." Once Scott traveled to Riversdale to attend a tulip bulb auction and stayed with his friends George and Rosalie Calvert (Callcott 1991:38,119). Scott traded seeds as near as Annapolis and as far away as the West Indies (Letzer and Russo 2003:200; Selig 2015:72). In fact, he even had a tropical tree shipped to him from Haiti (Selig 2015:72). The variety of specimens planted at Belvoir in the garden and greenhouse would have provided any visitor with an exotic experience. In addition to this visual stimulation, the plants and seeds were likely cultivated for medicinal purposes and used to treat his patient's ailments, including those he enslaved.

THE AMERICAN REVOLUTION

Although Scott is recorded as an upstanding citizen and respected physician, he was also a privileged colonist who bought and sold human souls. Some struggle with reconciling many American heroes' morality and slavery, whether it be George Washington or this affluent Irish immigrant doctor living in Annapolis. Indeed, these men left behind a celebrated legacy, led a country through wars, yet they were slave owners. The contradiction is uncomfortable, but colonial society was built out of the European invasion of America and the subsequent kidnapping of Africans to develop land stolen from Indigenous people. Scott, and his American colleagues and family, had an active role in sacrificing human beings for the growth of the colonies and eventually an independent country. In their minds, labor shortages and high wages justified their participation in the slave system. In Scott's own words, "the necessity we are under of employing Negroes is one of the most disagreeable circumstances attending a residence in this country, but as servants of a different nature can not be got when wanted" (Scott 1812a). This quote does not communicate his moral issue with enslaving people but his frustration with a labor shortage and the hassle of finding, purchasing, and managing human chattel. Initially, the colonies solved the problem with indentured servants, and promise of free land, but those attractions eventually dissolved leaving the aristocrats with a labor shortage; slavery was their imperfect solution to the problem. When the American Revolution arrived and blood was shed to defend what had been built, the colonies never considered the freedom of those who helped build this country. In the end, there was freedom from Britain but not freedom for all. When we discuss the American Revolution, it is important to remember whom Independence Day left out. Born enslaved in Maryland, Frederick Douglass proclaimed in a speech in 1852 "What to the Slave Is the Fourth of July," "The rich inheritance of justice, liberty, prosperity and independence, bequeathed by your fathers, is shared by you, not by me. The sunlight that brought life and healing to you has brought stripes and death to me. This Fourth [of] July is yours, not mine" (Foner 1999:200).

By 1775, the colonies' opposition to the British Crown began to grow, and Scott needed to travel back to Ireland to look after a paternal inheritance. Although not the best time to travel overseas, he was determined nevertheless and secured passage to England on June 6, 1776. He stayed for a period in Belfast before going to London. During this time, his wife, Elizabeth, stayed at Belvoir. She managed the estate and had some trouble. Right before Christmas in 1779, Tom, who was enslaved and worked in the manor house, fled Belvoir with "a light-coloured country made cloth jacket, with a red short waistcoat under it, a pair of light-coloured country cloth breeches; he also took with him a pair of leather breeches, dark coloured yarn stockings, and two pair of shoes" (*Maryland Journal [MJ]* 1780a). It was believed he ran back to Virginia, where he was sold away from his family as a small boy. The time around Christmas was the most opportune time to self-emancipate since enslaved people often secured passes to visit family for more than one day.

Although Mrs. Scott was without Dr. Scott for a few years, she was not isolated in the country; her widowed sister, Anne "Nancy" Ross Key, who had gone blind, and niece Elizabeth Key were likely either living or staying for long periods of time at Belvoir. In fact, Elizabeth Key was quite mobile during this time and traveled often to the Eastern Shore of Maryland courting with Henry Maynadier. They married at Belvoir in July 1781 (Selig 2015:29).

In the fall of 1780, Benjamin Franklin was called upon to facilitate passage for Scott back to Maryland. On his return, Scott requested to take an oath to the United States but was initially denied (Selig 2015:23–28). As such, he stayed out of politics and kept a low profile back at Belvoir. It is here where he encountered thousands of soldiers and the French commander Le Count de Rochambeau. At the end of the American Revolution, on the night of September 17, 1781, Rochambeau and approximately 4,500 of his men bivouacked at Belvoir. A map shows the approximate location of the troops on the west side of the road from "Scots House" (Figure 2.3). The only description of the site states that "we arrived at the location on a height we camped along the edge of the forest on a small hillside which looks over the small butchery behind the camp in the woods" (Belvoir Camp 1781; Selig 2015:35–36).

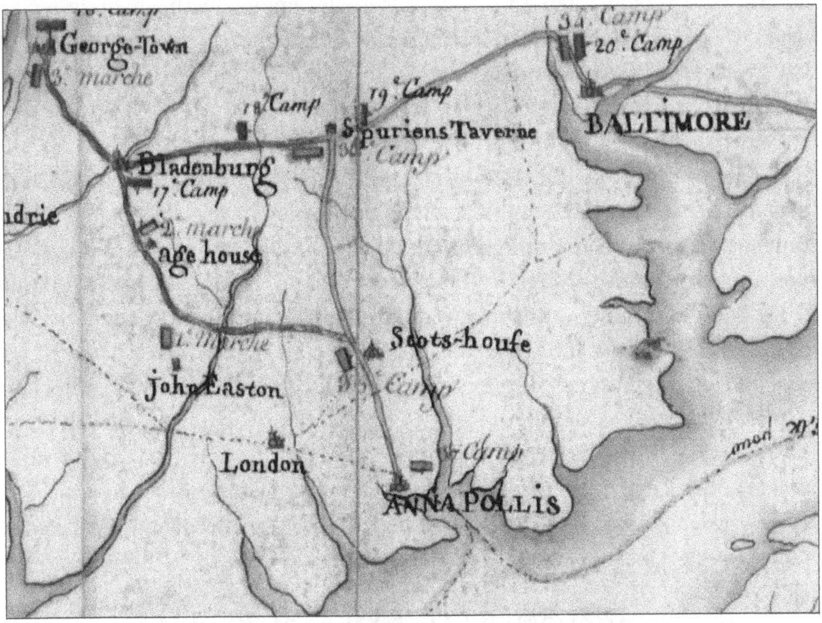

Figure 2.3. Section of *Côte de York-town à Boston: Marches de l'armée* map, 1782, showing "Scots House" (Belvoir) and the Rochambeau camp. (Courtesy of the Library of Congress, G3716.S3 1782, C6.)

There are many hills and rises around Belvoir, and, therefore, it is difficult to pinpoint the approximate location of this camp. There is no mention of outbuildings, only a butchery that may have been located downwind, south or east, of the manor house. Although much of Belvoir's surrounding landscape has been modified over time, a trace of the colonial road still hugs the west side of the stone manor house before winding its way south past the formal gardens, the Ross-Key family cemetery, and onto Annapolis. It is possible the soldiers encamped along this route since it is on the way to Annapolis and near freshwater, a necessity for the hundreds of heads of animals they rode upon and marched alongside. If they did stop here, it is unlikely archaeologists will ever find Rochambeau's camp. At the edge of the formal garden are numerous modern homes surrounding the old road to Annapolis, as well as the Ross family cemetery. To the southwest is a golf course with a spring-fed pond, perhaps a location where Rochambeau's men and animals may have stopped. This modern development, however, likely erased any subtle traces of the French commander's visit.

After the American Revolution, Scott continued to live at Belvoir during the summer, while wintering in Annapolis. In 1783, he was enumerated with 32 enslaved people: 16 were children, 7 were men aged 14–45, 3 females aged 14–30, with 6 older men and women (females above 30 and men above 45 years of age) (Federal Tax Assessment 1783). The increase in the number of enslaved people likely stimulated expanding the manor house and constructing the stone quarter.

Scott enjoyed living in both Annapolis and Belvoir, but he spent an unusual amount of time in the country until 1785. The reason for his long tenure at Belvoir after the American Revolution may have been related to his unresolved reputation among political peers but also an illness that continued to plague him throughout later years (Edgar 1912:274). Scott suffered from gout, and many of his letters mentioned this problem (Selig 2015:62–63). Unable to make the seasonal relocations and regular visits between his city and country estates due to failing health, he looked to Maynadier, his nephew (married to Elizabeth Key), to take over the operations at Belvoir in 1788. At this time, the estate supported the original stone and brick manor house, a brick barn (36 ft. × 24 ft.), a stone quarter for enslaved people (32 ft. × 32 ft.), a log quarter for enslaved people (20 ft. × 30 ft.), and a lathe corn house (40 ft. × 14 ft.) (Federal Tax Assessment 1798).

MANAGEMENT OF ENSLAVED PEOPLE

At the turn of the 18th century, at least 27 enslaved African Americans worked at Belvoir, with 17 of them between the ages of 12 and 50 (Federal Tax Assessment 1798). Scott held 10 additional enslaved people at his two-acre Annapolis home on Shipwright Street. Here, they served the family and maintained a large garden. The records show he sold and bought people and only freed one person. In 1803, he manumitted Jeremiah "Jerry" Tanner, who was described as light complected, 28 years old, and the son of Peggy, who was also enslaved by Scott (Anne Arundel County Manumission Record 1803). It is curious why he only manumitted one person out of the hundreds of people he enslaved across several decades. About two years later, he sold a 25-year-old woman, named Henny, to John L. Dickinson, but she self-emancipated a few days after the sale to join her family in either Annapolis or Baltimore (*MG* 1805a). It is unclear whether they ever found Henny. Among many enslavers, splitting families up was frowned upon for allegedly moral reasons. Since marriage was a Christian union to be upheld, they encouraged enslaved people to form their own communities, marry, and have families. Family is where enslaved people sought refuge and safety. Eventually, enslavers exploited these traditional unions and used familial bonds to psychologically anchor people to their estates. Self-emancipation became less attractive to people who maintained strong bonds with nearby family and friends. Scott knew this and passed along these tricks of the trade to his protégé and nephew Clotworthy Birnie.

As Scott continued to age, he considered how to distribute his property (and people). Since he did not produce a direct heir, Birnie, his Irish nephew, was chosen. This relationship grew over the years and included written correspondence with some discussions focused on the lack of fieldworkers. During this time, Chesapeake planters struggled to find affordable labor. When advising Birnie on how to run an estate, he often focused on the difficulty of finding, affording, and sustaining a workforce, stating:

> and to this must be added the expense of labor, which may be executed by indentured servants, if you can bring such along with you, or by hirelings whom you will not readily be able to engage, except for enormous wages, or lastly by slaves who can be purchased as the lot of from three to four hundred dollars for a young healthy stout negro man bred up to the labor of the field, women all for on a third less than man, and old and young both males and females proportionally in according to their respective ages and attainments. It may deserve your attention that I can from my own experiences assure you that unless you strictly supervise their conduct and rigidly enforce their performance of their duties, you will not earn from their labor enough to feed and cloth them. From this observation you must be convinced they go with little time to allow to the prosecution of any schemes of traffic, at least for some years to come after you have got your farm in good order and your people so well disciplined then you can place some confidence in their honesty and industry (Scott 1806).

Although hiring overseers was one way to force obedience and ensure that one squeezed as much labor as possible out of enslaved workers, they were not always a practical choice. When planters began to diversify crops, which simultaneously reduced laborers and increased skilled workers, it became impractical to hire overseers. Instead, planters devised other ways to attempt to manipulate their bondsmen into loyalty and a strong work ethic. Thomas

Jefferson, for example, eased up on his supervision of his enslaved people by overseers and allowed them to choose with whom they lived (Neiman 2008:185). The permission to pick housemates also coincided with a regional shift from barracks to smaller family cabins. Letters between Maynadier and Birnie also referenced the problem of enslaved African Americans resisting relocation to a new estate based on family ties. Birnie regularly complained about not having enough laborers, and Scott responded by mailing advertisements for auctions in Annapolis. Even Maynadier volunteered to purchase enslaved people on Birnie's behalf if he could not make it to Annapolis. During their labor search, Scott learned one of the men to be sold was between 30 and 40 years old, had a family, and was "represented by his overseer as a steady valuable hand" (Scott 1812a). Birnie never showed up for the sale.

Once Scott died, Maynadier continued to help Birnie secure enslaved laborers. Maynadier found a planter who "had two young negro men he would sell—-one about 18 and the other 21 years of age—both healthy—stout and brought up to estate business. Mr. Jacob Eigleheart owns those two and, believes one or both would be willing to go to you—as neither of them yet have wives to attach them to their own neighborhood" (Maynadier 1812). Of course, the consideration of whether they had wives was strictly noted to communicate the likelihood of successful relocation and adaption of these enslaved men to a new home rather than altruism. The economic loss of finding and apprehending those who self-emancipated inspired many enslavers to consider details about people's personal lives.

Scott proposed his own long-term solution for ensuring enslaved workers were faithful and hardworking. Since Birnie was a recent Irish immigrant, he did not possess the experience of managing or grooming a workforce for the future. With decades under his belt, Scott had some advice to bestow upon his uninitiated nephew: "I apprehend you will soon for the convenience of your children find it will be requisite to mix young women among your servants, whose children, educated inhabitants of industry and trained up in virtuous habits will acquire an attachment to your family and become extremely useful as they grow up; for this purpose a proper combination of the magisterial authority with kindness and friendly familiarity will greatly contribute if directly exercised in the general treatment of them"(Scott 1812a). Clearly, Scott was recommending a trusted avenue to increase the number of enslaved people by purchasing women who would naturally reproduce with existing enslaved men. Any children who resulted from these unions, Scott believed, would be raised on the estate and be malleable and obedient to Birnie's children.

Enslaved people resisted, despite an enslaver's best efforts to manipulate and control them. If enslaved workers attempted to self-emancipate or refused to comply in any way, they were often sold South to places such as

Georgia or Louisiana. When Pompey and Jenny left Birnie, they were quickly caught and imprisoned. Upon learning about their capture, Scott paid to get Jenny out of prison and feared she would be sold for leaving. He was concerned of her eventual disposition stating, "This circumstance gives me much uneasiness because Jenny's husband and daughter live with you it would be inhuman to separate them, if however, you can sell them, and deem such a measure prudent I shall not object thereto" (Scott 1812b). In the end, Jenny was sold, and Scott kept his promise and did not intervene, although he did criticize the low price Birnie got for Jenny. From these written exchanges it is apparent Scott and his family managed their enslaved workforce with little emotion or reflection on the morality of it. At the worst, they saw it as a necessary evil, a sacrifice required to enjoy the lifestyle they were accustomed to and deserving as privileged, newly minted Americans. Although some compassionate undertones can be detected in Scott's correspondence regarding enslaved people, these emotions were still self-serving.

FINAL YEARS

At the end of his life, Scott stayed in Annapolis where he turned away from politics and toward medicine. In this capacity, he cofounded the Medical and Chirugical Society of Maryland and served as president for two years (Selig 2015:72). Henry and Elizabeth Maynadier continued at Belvoir with Elizabeth's mother, Ann Ross Key. Although Mrs. Key moved to Terra Rubra in Carroll County when she married Francis Key, she returned to Belvoir to live with her daughter and son-in-law from the time of the American Revolution until her death in 1811 (Smith 1909:72–73).

In partnership with Maynadier, Scott experimented with the crossbreeding of sheep and black cattle (Howard Papers 1662–1919; Selig 2015:65). They exported beef and mutton throughout the first decade of the 19th century to places like York, Pennsylvania. One of their contracts included 200 pounds of salted beef for the U.S. military (Selig 2015:67). Once Birnie settled in Frederick County, the three of them focused on raising and butchering sheep at Belvoir. In one account, Pompey, enslaved by Birnie, herded about two dozen sheep to Belvoir for slaughter. Pompey was often mentioned in Birnie's letters running errands on his behalf (Maynadier 1814).

Near the end of his life, Scott was no longer flush with cash and needed to borrow money to purchase enslaved people. He even asked Birnie for: "Four hundred dollars to enable me to pay for a Negro boy I have purchased to put into my garden under a German gardener I have been obliged to hire" (Scott 1812c). Upon the death of Mrs. Key, Scott drafted his will and divided his property and 23 enslaved people between his wife and heirs. During this time, Belvoir supported a large two-story brick dwelling house, a kitchen, dairy, icehouse, brick barn and stables, cowhouse, sheephouse, cornhouse, and several other buildings including a "large stone building for servants" (*MG* 1816). It is unclear from his will whether the enslaved people resided at Annapolis or Belvoir, except for Sam who is mentioned as living at Belvoir (Table 2.2). This record is useful in showing the family units and an attempt by Scott to keep the nuclear families together after his death. Peg, a cook, is the only one associated with her position. She is also listed with her daughter and grandchildren and just under Sam who lived at Belvoir. I wondered whether they all lived in the stone quarter. Interestingly, only 7 of the enslaved people named in Scott's 1811 will are listed in his 1814 probate; 14 of the 21 names are new and belonged to men and women in their teens and twenties (Table 2.3).

Table 2.2. People Enslaved by Dr. Scott at Belvoir and/or His Annapolis Home on Shipwright Street, 1811.

Name	Sex	Notes	New Enslaver
Mingo	M		Elizabeth Ross Scott
Chester	M		Elizabeth Ross Scott
Old Dick	M		Elizabeth Ross Scott
Harry	M	Nanny's son	Elizabeth Ross Scott
Jenny	F	Nanny's daughter	Elizabeth Ross Scott
Peg	F	Nanny's daughter	Elizabeth Ross Scott
Sam	M	Living at Belvoir	Upton S. Reid
Peg	F	Cook	Upton S. Reid
Peggy	F	Peg's daughter	Upton S. Reid
Malvina	F	Peggy's daughter	Upton S. Reid
Henry	M	Peggy's son	Upton S. Reid
William	M	Fanny's son	Upton S. Reid
Esther	F	Lucy's daughter	Francis Reid
Lucy	F	Lucy's daughter	Francis Reid
Lydia	F	Lucy's daughter	Francis Reid
George	M	Lucy's son	Francis Reid
Nelly	F	Poll's daughter	Francis Reid
Harry	M	Polly's son	Elizabeth Reid
Toby	M	Polly's son	Elizabeth Reid
Poll	F	Polly's daughter	Elizabeth Reid
Pedro	M	Polly's son	Elizabeth Reid
Anne	F	Polly's daughter	Elizabeth Reid
Henny	F	Sarah's daughter	Elizabeth Maynadier

Table 2.3. Probate Inventory of People Enslaved by Dr. Scott at His Annapolis Home and Belvoir, 1814.

Name	Age	Notes
Annapolis		
Old Dick	78	Infirm
Mingo	58	
Charles		
Charles	16	Gardener
Peg	50–60	Infirm
Peggy	23	
Malvina	4	
Hanaey	2 1/2	
Milly	6 months	
Susan	19	
Frank	45	Diseased
Belvoir		
Nany	72	Infirm
Dick	60	Infirm
Sam	38	
Jerry	21	
Dick	18	
Harry	16	
Robert	9	
George	6	
Joshua	5	
Charles	3	
Bristol	6 months	
Poll	52	Infirm
Nanny	38	Infirm
Lucy	35	Infirm
Betty	24	
Mary	8	
Peg	14	
Priss	14	
Liddy	4	
Beckey	2	
Henny	16	

After the passing of Scott, Maynadier left the estate and turned his attention to the African Colonization Society (ACS). He worked alongside his nephew Francis Scott Key on an endeavor to ship people of African descent back to Africa. The ACS's mission was to create global racial homogeneity. This initiative claimed to provide free African Americans an opportunity to create a new colony in Liberia, Africa. In a letter to Maynadier, Key penned his current actions on filling a ship to be sent to Africa: "Mr. Ridout told you, I hope, all the African news. Is Shorter ready? & what sort of a Colonist would he make? Meade will be in Baltimore (he is now in Philadelphia) in a few days, to select as many as they will have room for in the Ship from that place. They take out with them the 12 captured Africans who are in Baltimore" (Key 1819).

The United States' aristocrats began to see an uncomfortable increase in the number of free Black people and fear set in. Key, Maynadier, and many others recognized the fallout slavery was leaving behind with significant social and economic disparities along with racial tensions. They believed sending free and enslaved Black Americans to Africa would solve many problems caused from raising a society dependent upon enslaved labor. From the African American's perspective, they identified as Americans and knew little of Africa, except from the oral histories, religion, and recipes passed down from their grandparents; they were American, and the United States was their home, for better or for worse. Not surprisingly, the ACS movement failed but not before the elite confessed that "free labor was superior to enslaved labor" (Lovit 2011:308). Unfortunately, for all of us, the ACS's 200-year-old epiphany was realized much too late, and we continue to struggle with societal ills left behind by America's racialization of slavery.

THE WORTHINGTONS

Brice John Worthington was a tobacco planter who owned over 2,000 acres of land and many properties in Anne Arundel County, including a stately brick home at the intersection of Duke of Gloucester Street and Conduit Street (179 Duke of Gloucester Street) in Annapolis (Maryland Inventory of Historic Properties 1983). He lived immediately adjacent to Belvoir at his estate called Summer Hill. Belvoir was on the market for months, and just about to head to public auction, when Worthington purchased it in 1816 for $25,000 from Maynadier who was managing the transaction. Interestingly, Worthington's wife, Anna Lee Fitzhugh, was Maynadier's niece (Warfield 1905:154). Additionally, both men were appointed Anne Arundel County justices of the peace by the governor in 1815 (*MG* 1815). It is unclear whether Worthington ever lived at Belvoir, but he did own and live at Summer Hill, adjacent to Belvoir, around 1815 (*MG* 1816). It is probable that an overseer or one of his sons or sons-in-law was operating Belvoir for him, or he may have moved to Belvoir and allowed other family members to occupy Summer Hill for a time. At his death on November 14, 1837, Brice was living at Summer Hill, while George Worthington, his son, managed Belvoir and his enslaved people. Eventually, the father willed Belvoir, along with human chattel, horses, cattle, sheep, hogs, and associated farming equipment, to his son George (Worthington 1837).

Within a few years, George sold the property to his brother-in-law, John T. Hodges (Elizabeth Worthington), before it was passed to Nicholas Brice Worthington, George's brother (Selig 2015:90). Despite the change in hands, George continued managing Belvoir's enslaved community through his overseer, Edward H. Brown. Here, the enslaved community included at least two nuclear families. Alley had two sons, Thomas and Moses, and two daughters, Sarah Ann and Harriet, while Lydia was listed with three daughters, Cinderella, Lucinda, and Eliza, and two sons, Basil and John Henry. Two men, Harry and James, are also listed together in Brice's 1837 will, but it is impossible to determine whether they were fathers of any of the children. Some of these people lived at Belvoir, possibly as early as 1816 when Brice purchased the estate (Worthington 1837). Although they were the only enslaved people listed in Brice's will, others may have been given to his children in advance of his passing. He confirms this in his will to his daughter, Elizabeth Hodges, stating, "all the property which she has already received from me" (Worthington 1837). Brice enslaved dozens of people, most of whom lived at Summer Hill, Belvoir, as well as his other properties. In fact, in 1830 he was enumerated with 80 enslaved people (U.S. Federal Census 1830).

The Worthingtons do not appear to have improved Belvoir's manor house or the estate at large. They may have built new, or repaired existing, outbuildings, but I have not been able to identify any construction dates from their tenure except for one brick outbuilding. In the front yard of the manor house, we found a square anomaly with ground-penetrating radar (GPR). GPR is a geophysical scan of the ground that can provide locations of buried features such as foundations. Using these data as a guide, we laid out and dug an excavation unit to determine the age and type of feature. The anomaly turned out to be a brick foundation from an earlier 19th-century outbuilding (Figure 2.4). The limited excavations did not reveal a function for the structure, but it could have served as a detached kitchen or other outbuilding.

Although George owned Belvoir, he also dabbled in other things, including religion and poetry (Worthington 1871, 1875). At the end of his life, he saw himself as a blind and disabled clergyman who suffered much in life. George admitted to relying on his friends and family to get by, as well as selling religious books including his own publication, *Sacred Poems*

Figure 2.4. Early 19th-century brick foundation feature in front (east) of Belvoir manor. View toward south. (Courtesy of the Maryland Department of Transportation.)

(Worthington 1875). In this final book of poems, he makes a plea for money so he can continue writing. Before losing all his property, he considered selling enslaved people as a solution to pay off his debt. The threat of being sold South was one of many inhumane tactics used to control enslaved people. George's grandfather Nicholas Worthington used iron collars for punishment. A 1790 ad described an enslaved man named Wat who had been a "waiting-man" until he was turned to labor in the field after "misdeeds while rifling abroad." "Had on, when he went away . . . an iron collar; but as he's pretty artful, he may get other clothing, and get his collar taken off" (*MJ*

1790). Elizabeth Worthington, who also lived near Belvoir and was perhaps George's great-aunt, submitted an ad seething with hatred for Phil who "was whipped on his backside the day he ran away, and very likely may have some scars there, is a vile rogue and one of the worst of liars" (*MJ* 1780b). From this ad it is certain Phil used every opportunity to manipulate his enslavers and resist them.

As mentioned, George enslaved Cinderella who escaped Belvoir with her husband, Abraham Brogden. They were caught soon after and George sold Cinderella outside of Maryland while Brogden spent three years incarcerated in Baltimore. The Brogden family continued to cause trouble for George. While Abraham was still incarcerated, Eliza, who had been working for George at his city residence in Washington, D.C., self-emancipated. Immediately, he put out an ad for $50, stating Eliza was "an intelligent servant, being able to read and write well, and may have papers prepared by herself" (*BS* 1852a). She was also described as being of medium height, stout, with a lighter complexion like her sister Cinderella. There are no further records about Eliza.

THE WELSH FAMILY

The Welshes were the last planter family to enslave people at Belvoir. Although historical records on Belvoir during this time are scant, I did locate some census and vital records. In 1825, Thomas Welsh married Elizabeth Sellman (Anne Arundel County Marriage Licenses 1825). Prior to Belvoir, they lived on a large plantation in Anne Arundel County along the South River with their sons, Richard and Thomas, and their daughters, Serina, Catherine, Ella, and Anna. It appeared that enslaved people regularly resisted their situation with the Welsh family by self-emancipating. During the 1840s, there was an uptick in the number of people attempting to leave Maryland, foreshadowing the unraveling of the slave system. This is also the time when Harriett Tubman and the Underground Railroad movement were organized, energized, and effective (Larson 2004). The stories of enslaved people self-liberating likely reached Belvoir and other estates, inspiring many to resist and leave for the Pennsylvania border and beyond.

When Thomas Welsh Sr. purchased Belvoir in 1850 from Nicholas Worthington, the buildings, including the stone quarter, were likely in need of repair. Although this building would have been solidly constructed by Scott, we learned through careful excavation of the interior that the building fell into disrepair over time. The corner brick hearths in the back rooms were haphazardly repaired several times; bricks were replaced and repositioned to accommodate cooking and heating. Eventually, the flooring became uneven; some bricks were replaced while others were pulled, exposing patches of sandy soil. The interior would have felt damp, and the enslaved household likely battled rodent and insect infestations. Belvoir was Welsh's second estate.

During the mid-19th century, Welsh grew a significant amount of tobacco compared to others. While he produced 38,000 pounds of tobacco, his neighbors were only growing several thousand pounds. Other estates, with a similar number of improved acres, diversified their crops by planting fields in "Indian corn" and wheat rather than tobacco (U.S. Federal Agricultural Census 1850, 1860). By 1860, Richard Welsh, Thomas's son, took over the daily operations of Belvoir and lived there with his wife, Lavinia Mills, and his toddler daughter, Elizabeth. Although his father may have lived at the South River estate (as insinuated by the census taker), his mother and adult sisters all resided at Belvoir. Richard's brother, Thomas, was attending medical school in Annapolis (U.S. Federal Census 1860). With six adults and a young girl, the manor house was a busy place. Over one dozen enslaved African Americans worked the 200 acres at Belvoir raising wheat, corn, and some tobacco. The federal census documented four horses, four mules, five milk cows, two working oxen, and five other cattle on the estate. In addition, 15 sheep and 20 swine were kept for wool and meat.

Over the next several years, the Welsh family rode out the U.S. Civil War at Belvoir. In 1863, Richard, who was still managing Belvoir, and his brother, Thomas, now a physician, were drafted to serve in the Union Army (U.S. Civil War Draft Record 1863). I searched the Civil War enlistment and pension records but did not find the Welsh brothers. Their absence from the records may be explained by a loophole in the military draft system. It was not uncommon for middle- and upper-class draftees to buy themselves out of service through either paying the U.S. government $300 or by hiring another man to take their place on the battlefield. In addition, sons who were taking care of widowed mothers, and even some married men, were found exempt from service (Levine 1981:827). Although Thomas and Richard appeared to have legally dodged the draft, they found themselves mourning the death of their mother in the spring of 1864. It is likely they were also becoming concerned about the future of Belvoir and if they could hold onto their human chattel.

On March 3, 1864, a story appeared in the *Annapolis Gazette* titled, "Negro Soldiers." It reported how a company of African Americans encamped behind St. John's College in Annapolis on their way to Baltimore. The article noted that both free and enslaved African Americans from the city and surrounding area enlisted at the camp. Allegedly, between 200 and 300 enslaved men from Anne Arundel County walked off plantations determined to enter the service. The newspaper surmised it was probable all enslavers in the county would find that most of the men would join the Union. There seemed to be little effort made to keep enslaved men from leaving the farms since the U.S. government claimed it would reimburse the owners at a price better than market value. Additionally, many believed emancipation was imminent, and there was no reason to fight to hold onto property with no value. The same newspaper article stated that "abolishment of slavery in Maryland is a foregone conclusion no one pretends to doubt"(*Annapolis Gazette* 1864).

Emancipation came to Maryland on November 1, 1864. During this time, 15 enslaved men, women, and children left Belvoir. A list of their names was compiled in anticipation of compensation by the U.S. government, but payment was never made to the enslavers. The people who walked off Belvoir included Ben Bacon (43), Andrew Thomas (34), William Crampton (34), William Tilghman (36), Nathan Brisco (18), Robert Crampton (15), Rachel Jackson (43), Priscilla Jackson (15), Eliza Thomas (45), Matilda Thomas (15), Mary Jackson (12), Ellan Jackson (6), Fanny Jackson (4), Georgianna Jackson (2), and Elizabeth Tilghman (52) (Anne Arundel County Slave Statistics 1864). Some of these newly emancipated African Americans sought out their family, while others looked for work in Baltimore, D.C., or Philadelphia. A few even joined the Union Army to fight against the South. Nathan Brisco, born around 1846 and enslaved by the Welshes, left Belvoir by the fall of 1864. He was a native Marylander, as were his parents; he stood 5 ft. 4 in. tall and was documented with a light complexion, dark eyes, and dark hair (U.S. Federal Census 1910). When he left Belvoir, Brisco found employment as a waiter in Baltimore, but at 23, he decided to enlist in the U.S. Navy for three years (U.S. Naval Enlistment Record 1870). While with the U.S. Navy, he served on the USS *Kansas* as a steerage steward (U.S. Civil War Pension Index 1861–1934).

At Belvoir, we found evidence of Union soldiers, particularly around the stone quarter. While surveying to the west, a metal detector operator recovered a piece of a Jefferson hatpin that would have been attached to a wool Union soldier hat. The copper-alloy eagle talon was just enough to identify the artifact. Indeed, this single object was thought-provoking; however, I did not consider the temporary occupation by Union soldiers until later. We identified one dozen Union buttons within and around the quarter. The most common buttons included four general service coat buttons (identified by a single raised eagle on the convex button front) and four infantry buttons marked with the letter "I" in the center. Interestingly, there were also two U.S. Navy buttons with a fouled anchor, a cavalry coat button with a "C" in the center, and a Connecticut militia button (Figure 2.5). These buttons suggest a possible Union troop occupation within the building between 1864 and 1865, a time when those once enslaved at Belvoir had already left to find their families and other opportunities. Despite searching through various archival records, I only found a few of the enslaved men from Belvoir enlisted in the Union Army, and this was after emancipation. So how do we explain the Union buttons in this context? Did this building, with its uneven flooring and questionable heating, function as a temporary barracks for soldiers after the Welsh's enslaved community left? Were Union troops detailed to watch the nearby railroad crossing? Or were they hired to assist the Welsh family on the estate after the enslaved community left? In her recollections of the Civil War, "Aunt Lucy," who was enslaved at an estate along the Severn River in Anne Arundel County near Belvoir, recalled being visited by Union troops. She said they never hurt anyone, but they took what they could eat, and she cooked meals for them (Federal Writers' Project [FWP]1941). It would have been likely for Belvoir, a prominent estate along General's Highway and the railroad, to be a stop by Union soldiers looking for food and rest.

Figure 2.5. U.S. Civil War buttons found within and around the Belvoir Quarter. *Top row*, two Navy buttons, Connecticut Militia button, and General Service button. *Bottom row*, General Service, Infantry, and Calvary buttons. (Courtesy of the Maryland Department of Transportation.)

Although some stayed behind, most newly emancipated African Americans walked off their estates in droves. Historians have researched the various reasons people left or stayed. The most significant deciding factor to leave the estate, at least initially, was to exercise the freedom to come and go as one pleased (Johnston 1987:5). The flexibility to go in search of a different job that paid better wages, to move closer to family, and to join communities where they felt safe under this "free," yet oppressive, new world resulted in a migration of people across the landscape. This did not, however, mean they decided to settle down and stay in one location after that initial move. Freedom looked a particular way to those who did not have it. It meant moving at will from one place to the next. It also represented making decisions, changing one's mind, and seeking new opportunities. Despite this new transient disposition, African Americans did not necessarily travel great distances. Poverty, limited knowledge, and confidence in travel kept many people "rural and southern" during the last half of the 19th century. By staying behind, they were forced to work as farm laborers or housekeepers for low wages. Those who left the county migrated to Baltimore or Washington, D.C., and found employment in the shipyards or in service agencies as waitstaff or cooks (Perdue et al. 1976:268). After the Civil War, these cities grew significantly, while other areas slightly declined. In fact, Washington, D.C., bypassed Baltimore in their Black population after 1860, growing by 223 percent (Johnston 1987:6–7,9).

By the end of the Civil War, Belvoir was a quieter place and a shadow of her former self. Since I have not been able to find any references for the estate at this time, it is unclear how it survived the following decade. The time after the Civil War was the Reconstruction-era since many farmers had to adapt to new ways of agriculture and a slave-free system. Richard Welsh gave up rural agricultural life. By 1870, he moved to Annapolis with his wife and teenage daughter. At least part of his time was spent living at 103 Main Street near the port. A stark contrast to his planting roots, Richard now worked as a lobbyist for the White House. While he moved into a political position, his brother, Dr. Thomas Welsh, eventually returned to the family estate with his new wife and family.

In 1873, Thomas Welsh Sr. died, leaving Belvoir in flux for two years; the estate was finally settled and given to Dr. Welsh and his sisters, Ella Iglehart and Anna Watkins. In 1887, the estate was sold to Anne C. Hinkley; then in 1891 it passed to James C. McCrum (Selig 2015:95). The next long-term property owner of Belvoir was Rev. Casimir Polyanski, a Lithuania immigrant, who purchased the property from McCrum's heirs in 1898. He never lived there but instead rented it out to family members. Polyanski sold Belvoir in 1919 to William Coleman Rogers. Eventually, Belvoir passed onto Archibald Coleman, who sold 228 acres of Belvoir to a developer, Johannes-Greco Inc. (Selig 2015:101–103). The manor home and the property surrounding the historic estate remain in private hands today.

Since the 1730s, Belvoir has been home to hundreds of people. When Ross lived at Belvoir during the mid-18th century, he held at least 38 people in bondage. They lived in log homes, above the kitchen, and in other outbuildings. As the property passed down through the generations the number of enslaved people at Belvoir diminished in number; this reduction in enslaved people was likely related to not only the wealth of Scott but also the reduced number of acres he planted in tobacco. When he passed in 1814, Scott enslaved 21 people at Belvoir, and another 11 at his Annapolis home. At Belvoir, they lived in two barrack-style buildings, one of log and the other of stone. When Welsh Sr. purchased Belvoir in 1850, the log building was likely inhabitable due to deterioration, but the stone quarter, albeit in poor condition, stood and continued to house enslaved people. In 1864, the Belvoir Quarter was abandoned but may have been temporarily lived in by Union troops.

Today, we only know the exact location of one of the homes for enslaved people, the stone quarter, just down the hill to the north of the manor house. Many archaeologists and historians have studied estate sites and poured over documentation and accounts of how enslaved people lived in the Chesapeake region. From their work, and from the study of what was left behind at Belvoir, the following chapters discuss the home and the artifacts associated with the lives of dozens of people who lived within the Belvoir Quarter between the 1780s and 1860s.

3
Designing and Housing

> The ends aimed at building Negro cabins should be: First, the health and comfort of the occupants; Secondly, the convenience of nursing, surveillance, discipline, and the supply of wood and water; and Thirdly, economy of construction.
>
> —VIRGINIA PLANTER, 1850 (BREEDEN 1980:129)

ENSLAVERS REGULARLY ENGAGED their fellow planters in philosophical debates on the most efficient way to organize their estate (Ellis and Ginsburg 2010). These conversations included how to construct and locate quarters to maintain health, ensure longevity, and encourage peak performance of human chattel. They published theories on best practices of cabin and barrack construction in widely circulated periodicals (Breeden 1980). Within these publications, enslavers loved to pontificate on where to situate enslaved housing based on topographical elevation and proximity to water, roads, trails, and fields. They also thought about how best to distribute individuals and families among the various buildings. Those who worked as domestics, for example, lived near their work. Attic space above kitchens and the manor house, as well as separate but nearby quarters, often held enslaved women and children. The enslavers housed field hands and general laborers near their work in more rustic accommodations (Morgan 1998:108–109).

CONSTRUCTION AND PLACEMENT OF HOUSING

The planter not only considered the location and functionality of workspace but also the visual effect of enslaved housing on the landscape. Their ideal arrangement was to situate the manor home on a high point to oversee their estate and property. In many cases, the quarters were placed behind or to the side of the manor house or even along the driveway, especially if the enslaver wanted to display their large labor force to passersby (Vlach 1993:21). If possible, estate owners constructed enslaved homes out of stone and brick to emanate their wealth while feigning paternalistic expressions of protection and care. Keeping orderly habitations was an ill attempt to mask the enslaver's role in human brutality (Ellis 2010:142–143,153). Belvoir was laid out in a similar manner with these same motivations.

The Belvoir Quarter was placed in a way that considered distance, slope, wind direction, and location to the manor home. The view from the front door of the enslaver's home during the 19th century included the terraced gardens, bay, and Severn River. The eastern terraced garden wrapped around to the south or right until it met the road leading to the family cemetery and eventually Annapolis. Along with garden and water vistas would be views of workspace along with a kitchen and smokehouse to the north or left out the front door. Beyond the detached kitchen and smokehouse and down the hill to the north was the stone quarter with a log barracks likely farther to the northwest. Barns and livestock structures were located down the slope to the west or behind the manor home (Figure 3.1). In other words, the Belvoir estate was organized with more pleasant views consisting of nature and gardens to the east and south, while the quarters for enslaved people and the agricultural outbuildings were placed down the hill to the north and west. The approach by land up the drive to Belvoir, arriving from Baltimore, would have taken the driver through the quarters and the livestock buildings before arriving at the manor home.

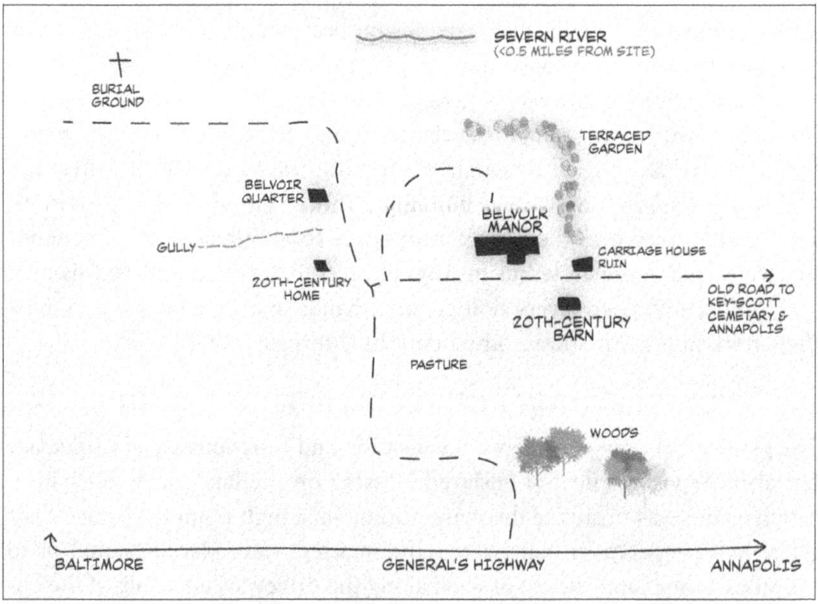

Figure 3.1. Sketch map oriented to the east toward the Severn River showing extant buildings in relationship to the Belvoir Quarter. Map not to scale. (Map by Andrew Bernish, Courtesy of the Maryland Department of Transportation.)

Although some of the people enslaved at Belvoir likely lived in outbuildings or above the kitchen, most lived in the stone quarter and a 30 ft. × 20 ft. log quarter mentioned in the 1790 tax record. While I confirmed the stone quarter location, we found a second eroded landscape to the west with domestic artifacts suggesting a historic home site. Based on artifact types and dates along with the location, the second log quarter site was likely here. It was also within view of the manor home and on the west side of a gully created from rainwater. This eroded channel was a shallow feature filled with domestic artifacts tossed away from the quarters as well as the manor home up the hill.

Enslavers also considered building placement and its health effects on people. They situated these dwellings close to water sources like creeks or ravines. If water was not nearby, they placed cisterns at the corner of the buildings to catch rainwater. This system would supply fresh water for drinking, cooking, and bathing. Often, they tucked quarters under a canopy of trees. If an existing overstory did not exist, they planted quick-growing trees to keep the sleeping area and workspaces cool in the summer months (Breeden 1980:19). Virgil Maxy, another Anne Arundel County planter, grew a stand of large locust trees for aesthetics but also to keep the home cool in the summer and warm in the winter (Hughes 1845:144). Enslavers believed rested workers and a tolerable temperature increased their efficiency and the likelihood of tasks being completed in a timely manner. These homes often had enough doors and windows to ensure ventilation and circulation of fresh air. Large barracks, for example, could have lattices for ventilation placed in interior walls between rooms (Hughes 1845:144).

TYPES AND SIZES OF HOUSING

Enslavers built and distinguished between the different types of housing, referring to single-family units as cabins and larger rectangular buildings as barracks or quarter(s). Cabins held a family of six while barracks sometimes held as many as two dozen people ranging in age from infants to the elderly; a loft increased capacity (Upton 2010:123). In the 18th century, it was not uncommon to see multiple enslaved families living in a 19 ft. × 35 ft. house with some of the quarters measuring as large as 16 ft. × 50 ft. (Morgan 1998:104–106). Despite the size, enslaved people had little to no privacy. During this time, enslavers considered duplexes as a housing option to accommodate nuclear families. These buildings housed two families and had a central fireplace opening to separate living quarters with two front doors (Morgan 1998:106,112; Samford 2007:89). Only about half of the enslaved workers lived in these types of homes. While the option for a single-family living space may have been a preferred situation, enslaved families continued to experience cramped space, no privacy, and unhealthy living conditions in log homes with dirt or wooden floors. In Maryland, considering the historically high number of enslaved people, there are relatively few surviving examples of these homes.

Most quarters were built of hand-hewn logs and fewer from stone and brick. The choice of building material was dependent on the wealth of the planter and the regional availability of stone and timber for construction. Although most quarters were built from locally felled trees with stone and/or brick fireplaces, some estates boasted duplex barracks, some even rising to accommodate two floors made from brick or stone. A Georgia enslaver, for example, preferred brick for his large quarter due to long-term affordability; brick buildings outlasted wooden ones and were essentially fireproof (Breeden 1980:125). If constructed from wood, the buildings may have sat about two feet above the ground on brick piers. This elevation kept the home off the damp earth and encouraged circulation and movement of air under the floor. Some enslavers believed this would also discourage the accumulation of trash under and around the homes. Often, overseers inspected the crawlspace and enforced the area to be free of debris (Breeden 1980:128–129). One ill-toned and racist account noted the stench that hung in the air of the cabins from the processing and consumption of food. The enslaver recounted he "found an accumulation of foul matter in layers almost denoting the number of years it had been collecting" under the raised area of the cabin (Breeden 1980:130). In contrast to such accounts is the cultural and archaeological evidence for clean and orderly spaces surrounding enslaved people's homes.

YARD SPACE

While at home, enslaved people actively lived, cooked, and worked outside in the yard. The yard space included the immediate area surrounding the home and gardens but excluded ancillary buildings farther away (Heath and Bennett 2000:38). Expanding living space to the outdoors provided relief from tight quarters that were poorly ventilated, often cramped, and dark. Furthermore, Africans and African Americans treated yards as sacred, private, and powerful spaces (Battle-Baptiste 2007:246). Since yards were used as extensions of the home, it is important to archaeologically investigate these areas for evidence of specific activities as well as changes of use over time. Although processing food, laundering clothing, and general socializing can leave artifacts behind, we often find the areas immediately surrounding the home clean (Kelso 1984:173–174; Fesler 2004, 2010:35; Barton 2022: 59–62). Yard sweeping, an activity originating in Africa, was believed to have been carried out on a regular basis and with vigor. From a practical standpoint, enslaved people would rake and sweep dried grass, brush, and other debris away from a home to prevent a structure fire, remove unwanted insects, and prepare areas for other uses such as laundry and socializing. Just as importantly, yard sweeping was a cultural activity and was common around African homes as a method to remove unwanted spirits (Thompson 1990:164; Heath and Bennett 2000:43; Fesler 2010:35). Psychologically, cleaning and sweeping also soothed anxiousness. While an overseer may have perceived this activity as compliance and obedience, enslaved people swept and maintained their yards for their own motivations and chose when to perform this duty. Some of those reasons included protecting their household against the enslaver and the negative energy swirling around them (Battle-Baptiste 2010:89–90; Barton 2022:64).

At Belvoir, I directed the placement of small and large excavation units around the stone quarter to understand how the yards were used over time. As expected, we found some artifacts in sheet middens (thin layers of artifacts), but the soil appeared eroded and disturbed by a septic drain field on the north side of the quarter. Already receiving runoff from the manor house and associated outbuildings, a large, braided drainage cut down the hillside just to the west of the quarter. Here, enslaved people tossed hundreds of artifacts into this shallow gulley to be washed downhill. While the eroded ditch terminated in a wetland behind the quarter, large pieces of mid-18th- through mid-19th-century broken wine bottles, ceramic plates, and other debris lodged in the sides and the bottom of this feature. Although our archaeological excavations within the yard space did not locate any features or obvious evidence of yard sweeping, the enslaved households living here through about 1850 kept their yards neat by tossing debris into this shallow gulley.

THE BELVOIR QUARTER

At least 15 years ago, Douglas W. Sanford and Dennis J. Pogue (2009) took on a multiyear project to find and record the homes of enslaved people in the Chesapeake region. Using the1860 U.S. federal census records, they estimated over 110,000 buildings served as enslaved households in Virginia, while Maryland only had 7,250 buildings. Maryland's low figure is a gross underestimate of the number of dwellings. It appeared that some census marshals only counted buildings used exclusively for housing enslaved people. While Anne Arundel County enumerated 1,018 enslaved households, for example, other counties neglected to count any. Indeed, the number would be much higher if they accurately counted the buildings and if they included attics, basements, and kitchens (Sanford 2022; Pogue 2023). Very few of these homes survive today. In Maryland, there are 237 documented "slave-related buildings." It is likely some of these structures are no longer standing. Another contributing factor for Maryland's low survival rate of enslaved homes may be related to limited field research and survey for these structures (Sanford 2022).

Upon emancipation, enslaved people living in the Chesapeake region vacated the buildings, allowing many of the homes to fall into ruins while those built out of brick and stone standing closer to the manor home were more likely to be repurposed and maintained (Pogue 2023). Perhaps the low number of extant houses is related to enslaved people leaving the estate immediately after emancipation. Did these Marylanders have more opportunities for work off the estate in nearby Annapolis, Baltimore, and D.C. than in Virginia? Perhaps the relatively close state of Pennsylvania with a large free Black community attracted others. If the farmers did not rehire tenants due to shifts in agricultural needs and practice, perhaps these wooden homes quickly collapsed.

The Belvoir Quarter is the only documented home for enslaved people with a *square*, multiroom arrangement in Maryland. Others existed, but they either survive as unrecorded historic homes or misinterpreted archaeological sites. This quarter measured roughly 34 ft. square on the exterior and 32 ft. square on the interior (Figure 3.2). It was either covered in a hipped or pyramidal roof with a centrally located brick chimney that opened into three separate rooms: two habitations and a kitchen. The walls are 2 ft. thick and constructed of red sandstone, also referred to as ironstone, and may have been tall enough to support a half story or loft above the main level (Figure 3.3). Lofts were uncommon in all quarters, but they were found in the Chesapeake region. The extra space above would have been useful for storing supplies and providing sleeping quarters (Morgan 1998:117). Although we did not

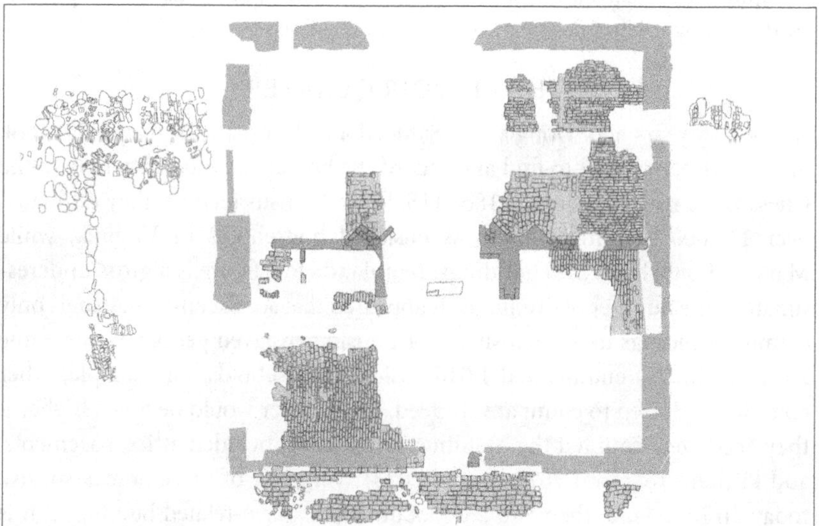

Figure 3.2. Footprint of the Belvoir Quarter showing interior brick flooring. (Courtesy of the Maryland Department of Transportation.)

find evidence of stairs to a loft or second floor, a ladder may have provided access to an upper room. The collection of archaeological samples of plaster and paint suggest the interior walls, along with the interior brick wall that divided the quarter in half, were finished and whitewashed.

Figure 3.3. Excavation of the Belvoir Quarter with exposed 1780s stone foundation in the foreground followed by a 20th-century concrete foundation and brick flooring. The row of cinder blocks on the right is from the late 20th-century tenant house. View toward the west. (Courtesy of the Maryland Department of Transportation.)

The quarter's front door was centrally placed on the south side and led into a 32 ft. × 15 ft. kitchen with a large brick fireplace. Here, the cook prepared meals for Belvoir's enslaved community. Just to the right or east of the fireplace was a doorway that led to a bedroom (Figure 3.4). It had a corner fireplace, and the room measured about 15 ft. × 15 ft square (Figure 3.5). In addition to the interior door, this room also had an exterior door that opened into the east yard. This bedroom could have accommodated several people and may have been used by the cook and her family.

Figure 3.4. Brick flooring leading from the kitchen into the northeast bedroom. Note the worn brick from feet scuffing across the threshold. (Courtesy of the Maryland Department of Transportation.)

Figure 3.5. Corner brick hearth feature with ash in northeast room. (Courtesy of the Maryland Department of Transportation.)

On the opposite side of the building, in the northwest corner, was an identical habitation that also had a corner fireplace and a single doorway that opened to the gently sloping west yard. It is possible this northwest bedroom only had wood plank flooring rather than brick flooring like the rest of the quarter. During the excavation, I did not observe any bricks and instead found the ground sloping away from the building to the northwest with water eroded gullies. In addition, I encountered a pattern of vertical nails sticking out of the soil, suggesting wood plank floors. Since this room only had an exterior door on the west wall, it functioned apart from the kitchen. As such, this room was likely occupied by someone who did not need direct access to the kitchen, but they may have held a higher-status position such as an overseer or valet. Generally, the higher-status positions on this type of estate included foremen or overseers. Although rare on smaller landholdings, the foreman would be primarily responsible for managing those who worked outdoors. The people in these positions could be free or enslaved, white or Black. If the planter was absent or lived elsewhere, the overseer provided an authoritarian presence over those who may attempt to resist through work avoidance or self-emancipation (Morgan 1998:218–219). At Belvoir, this person would have stayed either in their own cabin or a private room in a larger building. The northwest bedroom in the stone quarter was private with a window, corner fireplace, and a single exterior door.

We determined the placement of doors and windows from archaeological evidence. When the stone quarter collapsed, the walls fell outward, preserving the general shape of the brick surrounds of the doors and windows. On close examination, we observed that the stonemason lined the tops of the window and doors with arched bricks that tied into the stone wall. The windowsills and door thresholds were simply lined in plain bricks (Levinthal 2020). We collected hundreds of green, aqua, and colorless pane glass shards around the building. Glass windows provided lighting for working, while keeping out cold weather. In general, the iron fasteners were poorly preserved, but we still identified wrought nails and a few clinch nails used to join the door planks and secure strap hinges. We did not find evidence of shutter hardware. Pogue, an architectural historian and archaeologist, extrapolated additional details from similar late 18th-century buildings in the Chesapeake region allowing a realistic re-creation of the stone quarter (Figure 3.6).

The Belvoir Quarter was also a secure building. We found 10 lock-related artifacts and 3 keys. Specifically, we collected a rim lock, padlock, a keyhole escutcheon, and a key in the west yard adjacent to the quarter with a single padlock key cover on the east side of the house. Door locks and padlocks are

Figure 3.6. Architectural 3-D model reconstruction of the Belvoir Quarter based on archaeological evidence of the rooms, windows, and doors. (Courtesy of the Maryland Department of Transportation.)

commonly encountered on domestic sites, even homes lived in by enslaved people (Davidson 2023:900). Most of the locks we found were used inside of the home while the rim lock found in the west yard may have belonged to the exterior door of the northwest room. We also found a rim lock in the kitchen by the subfloor pit along with two keys. The southeast corner of the kitchen had a mortise lock possibly used for a chest or lockbox. The northeast room and possible cook's quarters had a rim lock and two padlocks inside. Davidson (2023:909) looked at 41 enslaved domestic sites and determined padlocks were more numerous (61%) than any other locking mechanism. The Belvoir Quarter had similar findings with slightly more padlocks (five) than rim locks (three). The discovery of locks in an enslaved context is psychologically significant and interpreted as a "moment of agreement" between enslaved and enslaver for privacy and perceived protection (Davidson 2023:940). The number of locks associated with the Belvoir Quarter confirms the enslaved household must have negotiated an arrangement with their enslaver to permit secured exterior doors as well as the interior door of the northeast bedroom. Since half of the home was a kitchen used to prepare and serve food, the enslaved cook likely used a mortise lock and padlocks to lock up knives and food to protect them from theft. In this realm, she possessed the power to organize, control, and manage this kitchen space. The limited freedom to lock and unlock the building's doors also provided her with control over who entered the building. These locks were either provided by an enslaver or purchased on their own.

When they abandoned the building, the walls eventually collapsed out and the rubble capped the soils adjacent to the Belvoir Quarter. By studying the artifacts under this stone and brick rubble, we determined the approximate time the building was abandoned and fell into ruin. The *terminus ante quem*, or latest date the quarter was occupied, is 1870. Under the stone walls, we found hundreds of domestic artifacts including broken stoneware, yellowware, redware, creamware, and various patterned and plain earthenware (see chapter 4). Some of the artifacts were related to food preparation and consumption and primarily dated to the mid-19th century, suggesting this yard space stayed relatively clean until the time the household enslaved by the Welshes moved in. Since the front half of this quarter served as a kitchen, the high artifact numbers and types of wares are not surprising. The window located on the west wall let in light and air to the kitchen, but it may also have served as an expedient opening to toss out trash. Household debris could also be thrown out the front door in a bucket, around the southwest corner, and slung into a refuse pile. Although the larger yard space contained fewer artifacts, the sloped area immediately adjacent to the southwest wall contained a midden, or collection of artifacts, from regular tossing of refuse into one area multiple times after 1850. The topography here facilitated the erosion of artifacts down the hill in front of the doorway of the northwest room of the quarter. The side yard would have also received refuse generated from the people living in this backroom. In fact, we found fragmented tobacco pipestems, a few buttons, and medicine bottles mingled with the kitchen waste. One of the bottles was from an amber bitter's bottle while another was an aqua medicine bottle distributed by Bartlett and Company on Calvert Street in Baltimore (Matchett's Baltimore City Directory 1853–1854). After the stone walls of the quarter collapsed, the stone and other salvageable building materials appear to have been taken and incorporated into other structural features around the estate, including a possible stone carriage house standing on the west side of the formal garden adjacent to the manor home. We also encountered disarticulated building stones along with an iron chisel (likely used to loosen the stones) in rubble adjacent to the quarter's foundation.

SIMILAR QUARTERS

The wealthy Chesapeake enslavers often preferred to keep enslaved valets, drivers, and domestic workers in brick and stone quarters while enslaved field laborers lodged in more rustic accommodations made of logs (Pogue 2002:4–5). Belvoir also followed this practice. Scott primarily housed enslaved workers in two barracks, one of stone, located closer to the manor home, and one of logs, likely situated twice as far away to the northwest. The size and dimensions of the Belvoir Quarter are reflective of housing seen in the Chesapeake region as early as 1770 and as late as 1843. The economic benefits of lodging

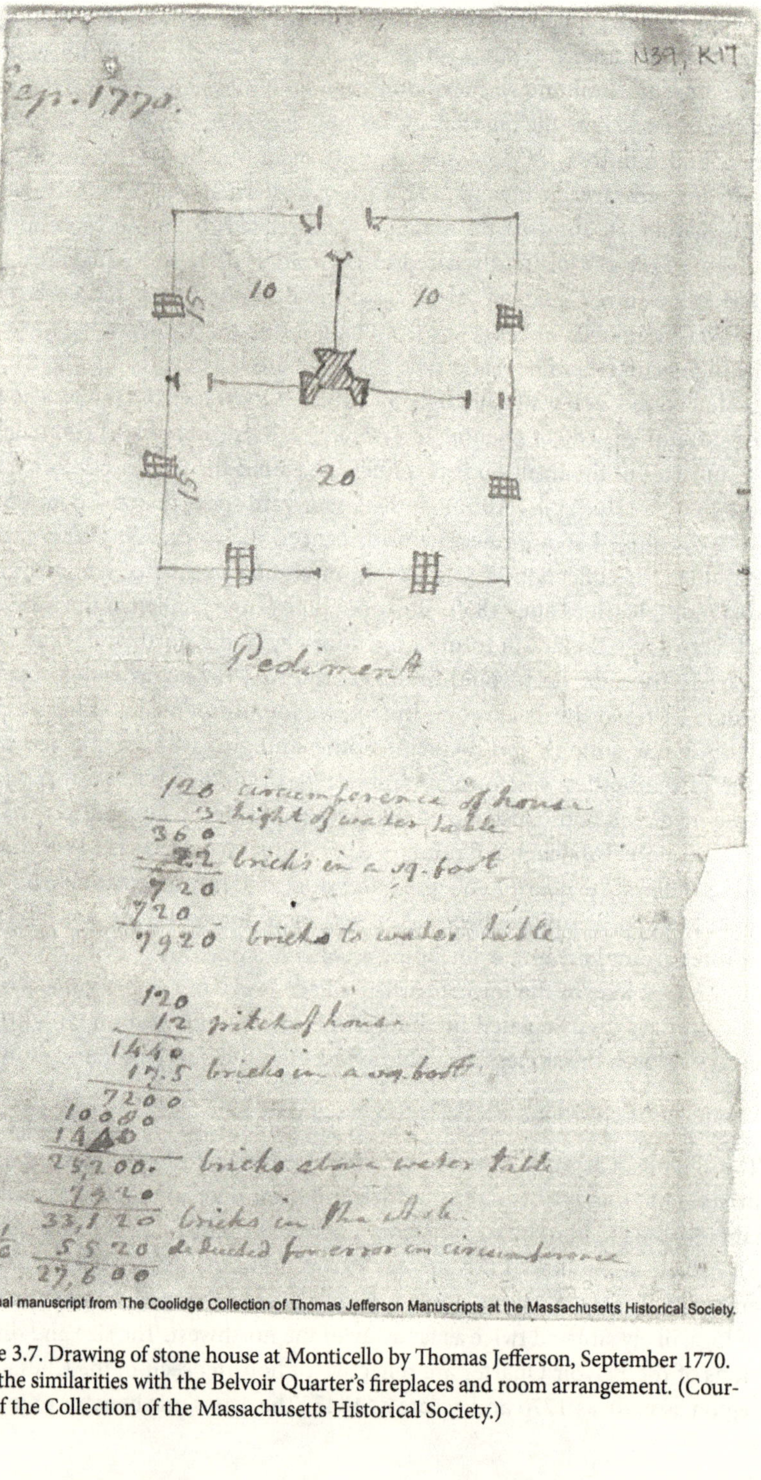

Original manuscript from The Coolidge Collection of Thomas Jefferson Manuscripts at the Massachusetts Historical Society.

Figure 3.7. Drawing of stone house at Monticello by Thomas Jefferson, September 1770. Note the similarities with the Belvoir Quarter's fireplaces and room arrangement. (Courtesy of the Collection of the Massachusetts Historical Society.)

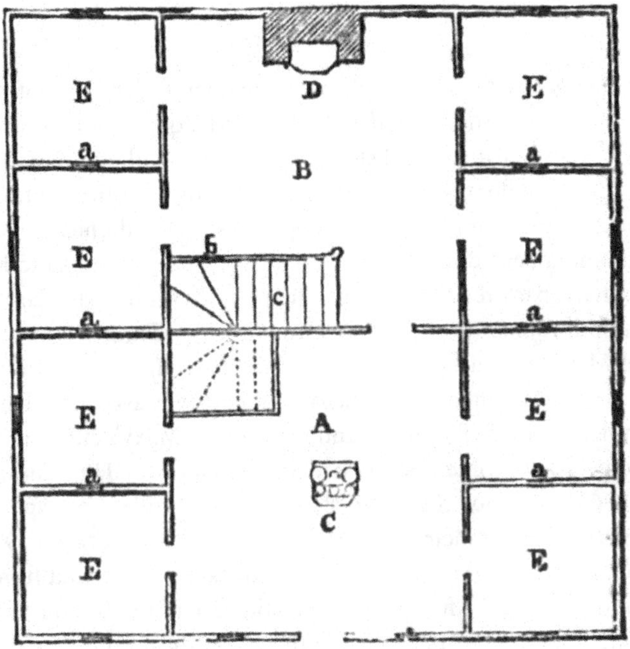

Figure 3.8. First floor of enslaved quarter built by Maxy: (*A*) kitchen, (*B*) living room, (*C*) cooking stove, (*D*) Franklin stove, (*E*) dormitories, (*a*) lattices for ventilation, (*b*) closet, and (*c*) stairs. (From Hughes 1845:144.)

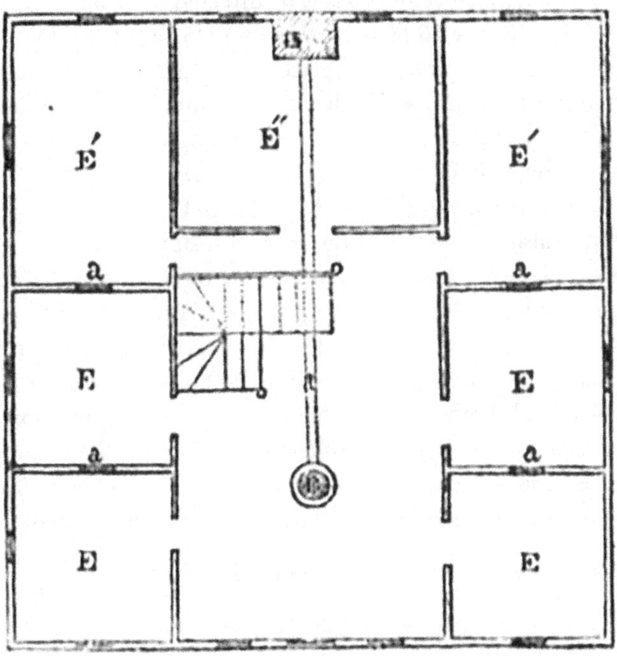

Figure 3.9. Second floor of enslaved quarter built by Maxy: (*E*) dormitories, (*E*' and *E*") family rooms, (*a*) lattices for ventilation. The center had a pipe and drum for heat. (From Hughes 1845:144.)

multiple people, particularly single men, together under one roof never went out of style. In fact, Thomas Jefferson designed a quarter that was very similar to Belvoir's stone quarter. Sketched in 1770, the building was 30 ft. × 20 ft. with a single front door that opened into a front room with a central fireplace. Jefferson designed the building to support two back domiciles with corner fireplaces and a back door that opened into a small entry area to hang coats and hats. Each back room had a separate private entrance that could support a family. Both rooms opened into the front kitchen (Figure 3.7).

Virgil Maxy, a wealthy planter who lived at Tulip Hill in Anne Arundel County, built two similar-sized quarters for his enslaved field laborers and their families in 1843 (Figure 3.8 and Figure 3.9). Maxy's father-in-law, Samuel Galloway, was a contemporary of Scott who was listed in Galloway's "Stud Book" (1763–1771) for his mare, showing the families corresponded with each other, at least for their horse-breeding business (Eareckson 1989). Maxy placed his quarters under a grove of locust trees with a well out front. The exterior measurement, 34 ft. square, is also the size of the Belvoir Quarter, but that is where the similarities stop. There are significant differences in the interior layout as well as the exterior materials between the two designs. Built on stone foundations, Maxy's buildings had wood siding with a cement first floor that supported two Franklin stoves. To accommodate multiple people, yet afford some semblance of privacy, he directed the construction of a second floor to house over 16 people (Hughes 1845:144–145). Tiny bedrooms, measuring about 8 ft. square, were placed adjacent to public spaces. The second floor supported additional bedrooms, including four larger dorm rooms used by families. The vacant space in the second story was used as a playroom for children and to dry clothing (Hughes 1845:145).

This layout is similar to military barracks and was allegedly designed for comfort but to also save construction and fuel costs (Hughes 1845:145). Other differences between the late 18th-century barrack designs by Scott and Jefferson are the building material and heat sources. These are temporal changes from the late 18th century to the mid-19th century in the preference of flooring, availability of lumber, and adoption of the Franklin stove for heating and cooking over brick fireplaces. Another difference in construction style may have been related to the type of workers who occupied the buildings. While Maxy was housing enslaved field laborers in these large buildings, Scott housed the enslaved cook and those who worked near his family and manor home.

HOME INTERIORS

With few exceptions, historic plantations consistently interpret homes of enslaved people as rustic cabins outfitted with the bare necessities. Whether one visits an estate in the Deep South or the Chesapeake region, the view into a cabin communicates enslaved people living in squalor without any semblance of domestic sophistication or luxury. The simple and homogenous depiction of these home interiors across regions is a result of few written historical descriptions on the daily life of enslaved households (Morgan 1998:114–115). Although the message of inhumane living conditions is correct, the oversimplification of these interior spaces is misleading and removes enslaved people's agency and unique lived experiences.

In general, the type of housing for enslaved people was dictated by their role (e.g., cook, field laborer, valet) on the estate as well as the wealth of the enslaver. The location and quality of an enslaved household's home could affect treatment by their own community (Galle 2010:26). Even the placement of people's homes on the landscape reinforced differences between enslaved individuals and families, and this created conflict. In fact, enslavers likely encouraged tension between individuals and communities as a method of control. The letters written by Scott demonstrate conscious coercion and manipulation of enslaved people to exert power over them. Providing upgraded housing and furnishings to some, and not others, was done with the intent to make enslaved people malleable and less likely to resist orders. While construction of the Belvoir Quarter from stone and brick created a more comfortable and healthy environment, it was primarily done to manipulate and control those who lived inside.

FURNISHINGS

Although the planter's architectural preferences and available material dictated the exterior of their homes, enslaved people still modified the interior space (Singleton 1995:124). Poverty, along with limited living space, meant they had few personal items, but improvements were made to increase functionality and comfort. Enslaved people either made or bought benches and stools for resting, while more finished pieces such as lock boxes, cabinets, and tables could be passed down from the enslaver (Katz-Hyman and Rice 2010:239). Fragile ceramic bowls, cups, and various sized plates would have been stored in cupboards and placed on shelves lining the kitchen walls. Open shelving provided inexpensive storage that facilitated the stacking of dishes and gave the enslaved cooks quick and easy access to their supplies. Large stoneware crocks and baskets sat on the brick floor along the walls, while yellowware and redware colanders, milk pans, and mixing bowls sat nearby.

Since wood is organic it does not preserve well in an archaeological context; therefore, we used metal pulls, escutcheons, and casters to identify the types of furniture in the Belvoir Quarter. Since furniture can be curated for decades, it is impossible to determine when a particular piece of furniture was used in this home. Regardless, a general understanding of the types of furnishings used provides a unique glimpse inside the home. We found a few hinges and escutcheons that belonged to lockboxes or trunks. In addition to storage containers, pieces of white marble and a cast-iron furniture leg suggest a marble-topped table stood inside. We also found a copper alloy knob or pull, likely used to open a drawer on a cabinet that sat in the southeast part of the kitchen.

The quarter was not filled with decorative ceramic bric-a-brac. Occasionally, an aesthetic ceramic form may have found its way to a shelf or the edge of a table to be admired. We only collected two pieces from porcelain figurines; one appears to be the face of a baby or small boy while the other is a child's leg against a tree. The only other personal furnishing was a thin copper alloy sheet metal fragment. This fragile piece likely belonged to a small leather case holding a tintype photo of a loved one. While the low number of decorative items may reflect poverty, it also suggests enslaved people did not participate in conspicuous consumption of ceramic figurines to communicate their individual tastes or to decorate their home. The choice may have been individual, cultural, or both. The low number of decorative pieces recovered from the Belvoir Quarter does not diminish the important function of the building as a homeplace and efforts to make it comfortable. The space still functioned as a relatively private refuge but may not have been seen as a place to communicate personal preferences and individuality through home décor. Instead, open shelves may have been lined with decorative bowls and cups displayed in a particular way to introduce color into the space. Furthermore, rustic wooden boxes and furniture, the cast-iron pots, and texture of baskets would have blended to aesthetically warm the environment.

SUBFLOOR PITS

Enslavers built quarters as cheaply as possible using recycled and subpar materials outfitted with the bare necessities. They also forced multiple unrelated people to cohabitate in one building resulting in minimal privacy. The human desire for discretion and confidentiality, however, can sometimes be detected in the archaeological record by studying the contents from small hand dug cellars, commonly referred to as subfloor pits. When a home was built, enslaved households used these pits as cold storage to keep food cool and preserved. Some archaeologists suggest subfloor pits began as borrow pits, where the builder used excavated clay to create mortar for the building's hearth and chimney (Kimmel 1993:105). An enslaver in 1850 noted that it was common to dig a hole under the floor and use the clay for mortar, but he discouraged against leaving the holes open since the enslaved household would use it to toss away refuse (Breeden 1980:121).

We have considered whether there are patterns to the numbers of pits per house, the time periods they were in use, as well as the evolution of pit function over time (Kelso 1984; Samford 2007; Neiman 2008). In the case of quarters and cabins, some archaeologists believe the size and number of pits are related to the composition of the household (Neiman 2008: 176–178). In other words, we should expect to find fewer subfloor pits in a family home versus a home with multiple individuals. If a family primarily used them as food storage, for example, it suggests the household was given bulk food and prepared their meals together. In this case, the dark space and coolness of the earth of a root cellar would help preserve tubers such as sweet potatoes, carrots, and other perishable foods. If an estate was organized to instead distribute prepared food to the enslaved community by a cook, in a separate and perhaps more central location, there would be no practical purpose for subfloor pits in the separate domiciles. This may explain why some homes lived in by enslaved people do not have subfloor pits.

Seldom exceeding 6 ft. in length, hand-dug cellars varied in size and could be square, oblong, or round. They were usually placed in corners but could be found in front of hearths (Samford 2007:112–113). We find these storage features in many modest homes across the Chesapeake region. Some posit that these pits are African in origins, but recent research suggests they are instead a New World adaption often found in mid-Atlantic quarters lived in by enslaved people (Davidson 2021). While relatively common in 18th-century enslaved housing, they quickly disappear by 1850 (Samford 2007:109–110).

Our method of excavation is meticulous enough to detect how enslaved households used and when they abandoned subfloor pits. Some appear to be immediately filled after use while others display multiple cut and fill episodes from repair and reuse (Samford 2007:47). Sometimes they installed wooden boards and bricks to hold back slumping soil caused by ground water or tunneling rodents. Wooden boxes could be nailed together to shore up the sides; some even had dividers for organization. Hinged doors or loose boards could cover the pits to protect the contents inside and keep people from undermining the walls through foot traffic along the edges.

As a comparison, Booker T. Washington (1901:5), born enslaved in Franklin County, Virginia, later recalled one of these storage pits in his cabin: "In the centre of the earthen floor there was a large, deep opening covered with boards, which was used as a place in which to store sweet potatoes during the winter." With little privacy or ways to protect personal items from theft, subfloor pits could also function as temporary storage space for knives, tools, or other personal items. Many of the quarters housed enslaved people who were not family or friends. Although subfloor pits placed in the kitchen stored food, individuals or families dug smaller holes to hold personal items. These pits could also hide stolen items such as food, tools, or personal belongings (Samford 2007:139).

We have also encountered objects and groupings of items within subfloor pits related to West African spirit practices. Once a hand-dug cellar stopped functioning as cold storage, the hole could be repurposed for many things, including a religious shrine (Samford 2007:149–173; Lucas 2014). These subterranean spaces would have been out of sight and convenient. If someone wanted to practice a religion that ran counter to an enslaver's beliefs, they used secret spaces to hide evidence of these rituals. Practitioners from West Central Africa, for example, believe *minkisi* (*nkisi* singular), containers holding spirit and medicine, can occupy an object or group of objects and protect the household. The spirit bundles often contain glass or quartz, brick pieces, buttons and/or straight pins, nails, white ceramic sherds, and other items. The original function of the artifact is not what is important. Instead, the material and colors of the objects are what empower the nkisi. People who practiced these rituals usually enlisted the help of a conjurer or healer who created the bundle and placed it near a hearth, within the base of a fireplace, or in corners of the home, with a deliberate intention to invoke the protective power of deities and ancestors (Leone 2005:199–244; Schablitsky 2012; Lucas 2014). A new hole could be dug to conceal the nkisi or an abandoned subfloor pit could have functioned as an expedient pit for the spirit bundle. At an early 18th-century quarter site near Williamsburg, Virginia, archaeologists dug into a subfloor pit and found an iron hoe, wine bottle body fragment that contained eggshell and bone, a clay tobacco pipestem, brick, black cobble, and a raccoon mandible believed to have been related to West African spirit practices (Samford 2007:157–158). At the former Anthony Thompson Farm, where Harriet Tubman was born on Maryland's Eastern Shore, we found a cluster of artifacts buried in a quarter's cellar in front of the fireplace. The bundle included ceramic sherds with blue glaze, a heart-shaped glass bottle stopper, a copper alloy button, brick, oyster shell, and ferrous nails. An enslaved person likely had the nkisi placed there to protect the home from negative energy.

BELVOIR'S SUBFLOOR PITS

The Belvoir Quarter's kitchen had a large hand-dug cellar placed to the west or left of the fireplace filled with a variety of household artifacts dating to the late 18th through mid-19th centuries (Figure 3.10). This subfloor pit measured 2 ft. (north to south) by 4 ft. (west to east) and 2 ft. deep. Although the original interior walls of the pit may have been lined in wood, there was no archaeological evidence for this. The small hand-dug cellar was likely created during or soon after the construction of the building; however, it eventually failed and loose bricks were used to shore up the walls. During the excavation, we found a trench cut through the subfloor pit for a waterline. The waterline serviced the small 20th-century tenant house that sat on top of the quarter's foundation before we removed it to access the archaeological site. The disturbed soil filled around the water pipe was processed separately and not associated with the subfloor pit. While this feature had been impacted, enough of the soil survived to determine how the pit was used over time.

Figure 3.10. Excavated subfloor pit on west side of kitchen hearth. The interior brick wall is shown as well as repositioned brick flooring that lined the south edge of the subfloor pit. A small pit containing bone, including a chicken head, was found south (right) of these bricks. (Courtesy of the Maryland Department of Transportation.)

Sometime before 1815, the enslaved household determined the cellar was failing. They abandoned it and filled it with refuse including discarded animal bones and ceramic sherds. Once the subfloor pit was filled, they excavated two smaller pits adjacent to it and eventually filled them with refuse. By this time, the brick flooring had been pulled up in this area of the kitchen exposing sandy soil. The first small pit (Feature 69) they dug was circular and measured 1.7 ft. in diameter and about 0.8 ft. deep. Once this hole was filled with household debris, a second small pit (Feature 67) measuring 2.1 ft. (north to south) and 1.5 ft. (west to east) was dug 2.25 ft. deep. It partially impacted Feature 69 and contained similar artifacts. The artifacts include late 18th- and early 19th-century ceramics, wrought and cut nails, aqua and olive bottle glass, oyster shell, and animal bones. Interestingly, I found a chicken head in each of these smaller pits. Chickens were commonly killed and butchered outside by removing the head. It is possible these expedient holes held evidence of the household's clandestine activities. Historic accounts often recounted enslaved people taking chickens in the middle of the night and hiding evidence of the animal inside the home (Savitt 2002:97).

When the Worthingtons bought Belvoir in 1815, a new enslaved community moved in and cleaned out at least half of the main subfloor pit and began to reuse it for refuse. They left the two smaller pits (features 67 and 69) alone and set a row of bricks on top of them to create an edge for the kitchen's larger subfloor pit. Resembling piano keys in design, this row of bricks may have facilitated the placement of wooden boards on top of the subfloor pit. Although the western wall of the pit had collapsed, we found a few stacked bricks on the inside and about one dozen others laid in a haphazard fashion at the floor level. The types of artifacts thrown, swept, and lost during the occupation of the second enslaved household included small personal objects, household items, and food remains. Most of the nonfood items included broken ceramics, glass, various iron fragments, as well as personal items (Table 3.1). The two enslaved households filled the subfloor pit three times, dug it out twice, and continually repaired it (Features 39, 47, and 49). The use of subfloor pits for purposes other than cold storage should also be interpreted as acts of resistance by those who built, used, and maintained them. The enslaved household understood use of hand dug-cellars for waste disposal was discouraged by enslavers and overseers, yet they used them anyway.

Table 3.1. Artifact Types Found in the Kitchen's Subfloor Pit.

Ceramics	**Glass (color)**	**Hardware & Tools**	**Clothing/Personal**	**Other**
Pearlware	Aqua	Wrought nails	Flat metal alloy buttons	Gunflint/strike a lights
Creamware	Olive	Bone handles	Bone buttons	Iron bars and strapping
Porcelain	Colorless	Knives	Straight pins	Lead bird shot
White refined earthenware	Blue	Axe head	Clay tobacco pipes	18th-century coins
Wieldon		Hinge	Beads	
Redware		Iron spike	Buckle	
English brown			Shoe buckle	
Tin glazed				

When Welsh purchased Belvoir in 1850, a third enslaved community moved into the quarter, but they never used the subfloor pits and left them filled with the refuse from the previous occupants. Instead, they tossed most of their debris on the west side of the building. While this is an area just under the kitchen window and west of the front door, this space could have been seen from the manor home and from approaching visitors. Perhaps brush or trees shielded the view from others, and maybe the slope was steep enough to hide the trash. When the west stone wall fell around 1870, many of these artifacts were trapped beneath the rubble. Both the subfloor pit and this capped mid-19th-century feature produced a variety of ceramic sherds. Although most of the assemblage was too small to determine vessel size and type, we identified many patterns and decorative applications in the collection. This ceramic assemblage provided interesting avenues of inquiry and urged us to consider alternate uses and interpretations of European-made ceramics by African-descended households.

4
Cooking and Serving

> The husband and wife sleep on a mean pallet; the children on the ground; [there is] a very bad fireplace, some utensils for cooking, but in the middle of this poverty, some cups and a teapot.
>
> —Niemcewicz 1965:100

The front half of the Belvoir Quarter functioned as a large, brick-floored kitchen and measured 32 ft. × 15 ft. with a central fireplace for cooking. Although 20th-century construction obliterated most of the brick hearth, archaeological evidence of its location survived as a partial chimney cheek base, a centrally placed rounded boulder, and reddened soil and ash. In the southwest corner of the room, the brick flooring showed scrape and spall marks suggesting a workspace, while the northwest corner of the room held the subfloor pit. The interior stone walls were plastered and whitewashed. Glass windows were placed on the west, east, and south walls allowing ample light for working. The kitchen had space for tables, storage boxes, and barrels; it could have also accommodated a sleeping area. The kitchen was likely outfitted with cast-iron kettles where stews and soups would have simmered over an open fire. Stoneware crocks sat on the floor while the enslaved cook placed her redware jars, wooden trays, and bowls on tables during food preparation. She served meals on white ceramic plates and bowls, while beverages were drunk from mugs and tea wares. These women prepared countless meals in this space, and evidence of their work was left behind in hundreds of pieces of broken ceramic plates, platters, cups, mugs, and bowls scattered around the site.

Ceramic sherds are some of the most diagnostic and interesting artifacts we collect from archaeological sites. The rapid evolution of decorative styles, techniques, and patterns on ceramic vessels allows us to date each sherd. Published chronologies provide the history of the potteries and time periods when decorative styles and patterns were produced and distributed; however, we cannot always determine when the plate entered the archaeological record. A transfer-printed cup made in the early 19th century, for example, may have not been broken and thrown out until 1850. As such, we need to rely on disposal patterns on the site along with other dateable artifacts to provide a time range of use and occupation by the people we are studying. Although the manufacturing date for our ceramic assemblage spanned over 200 years, these pieces were only used and discarded over about 80 years. Combining historical records and artifact manufacture dates helps us narrow down which households created an archaeological deposit, allowing us to match specific artifacts with certain groups of people. Inspired by other archaeologists, I considered how Belvoir's enslaved households acquired these household goods and why they may have chosen specific dishwares over others.

EVERYDAY CERAMICS

Although ceramic types used within the Belvoir Quarter included many utilitarian redware and stoneware crocks and bowls, there were also a high number and variety of inexpensive, yet colorfully decorated creamware (cream- or vanilla-colored clay) and white earthenware (whiter and brighter clay) pieces in the assemblage. The enslaved households used many kinds of hollowwares (e.g., cups, bowls, and mugs) and flatwares (e.g., platters and plates) decorated with painted floral designs, bands, and various abstract designs associated with dipped wares (also known as industrial slipware and mocha) and transfer-printed scenes. Other decorative earthenware pieces found here include edge-decorated platters and plates impressed with feathered and wavy lines colored with green or blue glaze along the interior rims. Edge-decorated platters and plates are very common on all archaeological sites across the United States from the 18th through 19th centuries. The presence of intricately decorated plates in the archaeological record communicates necessity and access to mass-produced dishware not affluence or privilege. We found very few ceramic sherds associated with pieces considered rare or expensive. Most of the ceramic assemblage represent dishwares commonly found on domestic archaeological sites throughout the Chesapeake region.

A variety of plates, tea sets, mugs, and other ceramics arrived in the hands of the enslaved community in different ways. The enslaver likely supplied some dishware, while the enslaved household likely purchased pieces from local stores or received them as gifts. They earned money through selling crafts, produce, eggs, or meat products to neighbors, enslavers, or people in Annapolis. Extra income could be earned from additional duties or for a job well done, particularly for those who held an elevated status and worked close to the manor house (Heath 2004:30–31; Galle 2010:26). At Belvoir, Pompey was given "a trifle" for having "performed his duty well" (Maynadier 1814). Within the Belvoir Quarter, we found 10 coins, in one cent and half-cent, denominations most dating to the 18th century. These lost coins suggest the enslaved households actively earned additional income to purchase a variety of items including ceramics. The quality, decoration, and function of the cup or plate were chosen, in at least some cases, by the enslaved and were likely based on cost, durability, color, and decoration. While ceramics are common in the homes of many people, regardless of class, the assemblages from enslaved households seldom belonged to a matched set (Wilkie 2000:15; Bloch and Agbe-Davies 2017:135). Influenced by Robert Farris Thompson's (1993) work, Wilkie and Farnsworth (2005: 273–277) call attention to African aesthetic traditions, including colorful artistry, and how this creative style may influence choice in ceramics. They wondered whether the symbols and patterns seen in African textiles motivated enslaved households to choose ceramics displaying similar designs and colors. Dipped wares, including mugs, bowls, and pitchers, display contrasts of light and dark colors along with geometric repeating patterns similar to African textiles. This ceramic type includes mugs or bowls as well as pitchers decorated with a variety of creative glaze application techniques, rouletting, and banding.

We found the same type of dipped wares at the Belvoir Quarter. The 262 sherds in our artifact assemblage represented bowls and mugs dating between the late 18th century through the mid-19th century. Most pieces contained bands in earthen tones such as brown, black, blue, green, and white. I did not attempt to calculate color preferences because the sherds were so small. Caribbean archaeologists, however, have looked at color, specifically banded dipped wares and polychrome-painted hollowware, and noted a higher number of brown and green glazes from enslaved contexts (Wilkie and Farnsworth 1999:308). While Belvoir's enslaved households used primarily banded dipped wares, they also drank and ate from dipped wares decorated with rouletting (incised lines) as well as cable patterns and dendritic designs (Figure 4.1).

Printed ceramics (transfer-prints) are designed with exotic scenes and natural landscapes including trees, structures, animals, and people (Figure 4.2). The Belvoir Quarter contained flatware and hollowware sherds decorated in blue, black, red, purple, brown, and green colors. Most of the ceramic sherds, however, were decorated in blue and brown floral patterns, scenes or landscapes, and geometric patterns. The enslaved household used a fair number of dishes decorated with the Caledonian pattern (1836–1842) resembling a Scottish tartan (Brooks 1997:44–45). Other patterns included the Dam and Waterworks (1815–1840), Persians pattern in blue by Samuel Barker and Son (1834–1893), and the Asiatic Plants pattern (1830–1834) (Crowl et al. 2022:268). Inspired by Wilkie and Farnsworth's (2005) observations on dipped wares, it is possible the Caledonian pattern ceramics may have been chosen by the enslaved household because of its textile-inspired pattern as well (see Figure 4.2). Instead of Scotland, they may have seen Africa. The boxed patterns and lines along with the blue color may have appealed to them over other transfer-printed patterns with romantic and pastoral scenes depicting whiteness.

Figure 4.1. Variety of decorative dipped ceramics representing bowls and mugs, a striped pitcher (*far right*), cable pattern (*bottom left*), and dendritic design (*bottom center*). These colors and patterns are similar to those in West African textiles. (Courtesy of the Maryland Department of Transportation.)

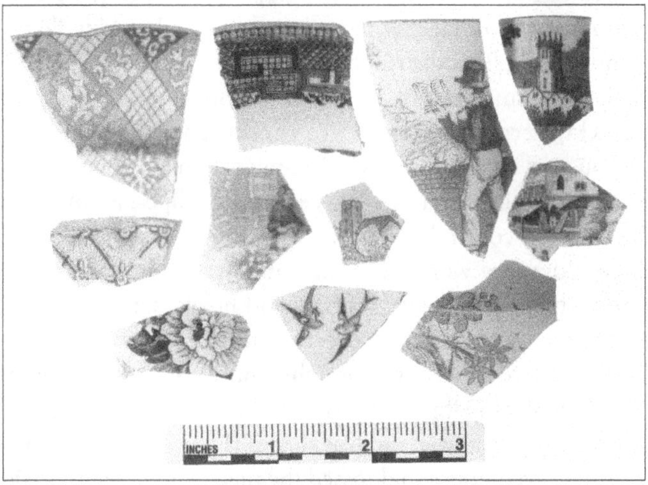

Figure 4.2. Variety of transfer-printed ceramic saucer and cup sherds dating from the first half of the 19th century, *top row, far left*, the Caledonian pattern in blue. (Courtesy of the Maryland Department of Transportation.)

Although dishware could be chosen on the general aesthetic of the design, enslaved people may have bought a piece based on spiritual symbolism. Images of birds or shapes could hold cultural meanings that resonated with a person of African descent (Wilkie and Farnsworth 1999:309). Birds, specifically, are often seen in West African cultures and associated with spirits and deities (Thompson 1983; Wilkie and Farnsworth 2005: 279). While some of the ceramic patterns and colors may have been preferred, it is unlikely all the ceramic vessels held in the hands of Belvoir's enslaved people resonated with them. We collected one cup sherd printed in black with a man wearing a top hat, reading a book with a church in the distance. On another ceramic fragment there was a man with a fur hat in an action scene with his arm raised, while other fragments show scenes printed in blue with a tower house on one and a woman near a fence with a house in the backdrop. Perhaps in some cases, functionality outweighed symbolic designs and individual preferences.

We often recover floral painted designs on white earthenware ceramics on middle- and lower-income house sites. Around the Belvoir Quarter, we found numerous cups and bowl fragments decorated with sprig-painted flowers in reds and greens, bold and fine brush strokes depicting blue flowers, and a variety of other floral designs in various colors; many have a concentric line around the exterior of the piece (Figure 4.3). The most common floral designs in our collection display at least three or more colors. Blue-colored bowls and cups are the most numerous, followed by pieces painted with natural shades of brown and green. Although fragmentary, we determined that polychrome or multiple-colored ceramics as well as blue floral designs were most numerous. This distribution is likely a result of availability of the wares as well as the small size of the sherds (Figure 4.4).

Other quickly decorated and relatively inexpensive hollowware found at the Belvoir Quarter included sponge-decorated wares. Potters took sponges, sometimes cut into shapes of flowers, geometric shapes, animals, and stars, dipped them into a colorful glaze and applied the designs to white earthenware pieces. The area within and surrounding the quarter contained 108 sherds belonging to plates, cups, saucers, and bowls decorated in this technique. We could only identify just over one-third of the fragments to vessel type; 44% represented bowls or cups, while only 18% represented plates or saucers. The designs were limited to basic and open sponge applications with a few sherds displaying flower and leaf shapes (Figure 4.5). Once broken beyond use, the enslaved household tossed the pieces along the west side of the quarter; the sherds date between 1820 and the 1860s, the period when the Worthington and later the Welsh families lived at Belvoir.

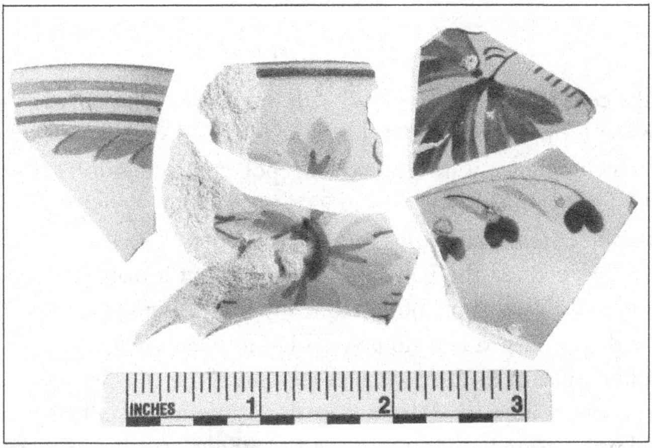

Figure 4.3. Variety of painted cup, bowl, and small plate fragments. (Courtesy of the Maryland Department of Transportation.) Transportation.)

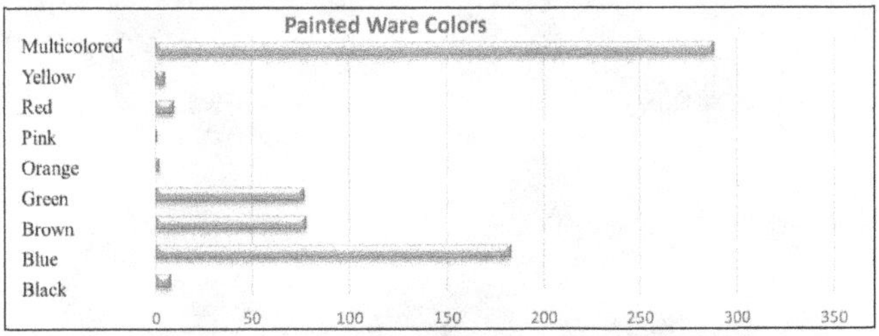

Figure 4.4. Number of painted ceramics sherds, by color. (Courtesy of the Maryland Department of Transportation.)

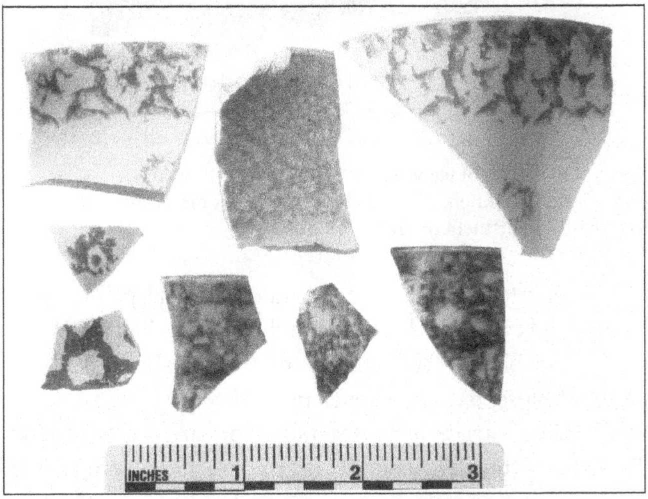

Figure 4.5. Variety of sponge-decorated plate, cup, and bowl sherds. These are commonly found in homes of enslaved people across Maryland. (Courtesy of the Maryland Department of Transportation.)

TEA WARES

Most of the ceramic sherds associated with the Belvoir Quarter were too small to determine form; however, 400 sherds belonged to plates, bowls, and serving pieces including tea ware (teapot/coffeepot, cup, and saucer) (Keim 2020) (Figure 4.6). Just about one-quarter, or 23% (96 sherds), served as teacups, saucers, or teapots. Almost all the tea ware sherds represented teacups, suggesting the cups either entered the Belvoir Quarter without a matching saucer and/or the household used cups more frequently increasing the likelihood of being dropped or damaged beyond use. A high number of cups without saucers would not be unusual in this context, especially if the cups were being traded between people, being passed down from the manor home, or being purchased at reduced prices from local stores for being without a saucer for example.

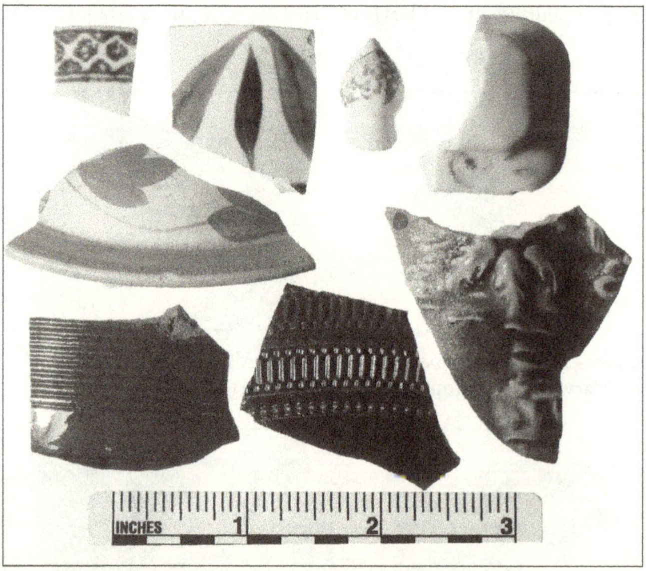

Figure 4.6. Variety of tea ware ceramics representing cups, sugar or creamer lids and knob, as well as teapot body sherds. (Courtesy of the Maryland Department of Transportation.)

The Belvoir Quarter tea wares are decorated in floral-painted polychrome, an inexpensive and common decorative technique applied in yellows, greens, browns, reds, and blue to the exterior of the cups and saucers. The enslaved household also passed transfer-printed teacups and saucers around their home. While a variety of scenes and colors are represented in the collection, blue floral transfer-printed patterns are most common. Although the sherd count on teapots/coffeepots was relatively low at just 20 sherds, there were well over one dozen vessels represented on the site. The enslaved households who lived in the quarter during the late 18th through early 19th centuries poured tea from Asbury-type, creamware, white salt-glazed stoneware, black basalt stoneware, Jackfield-type, and refined redware pots. The presence of expensive teapots, represented by the black basalt stoneware and white salt-glazed stoneware, is significant in this home. How did these pots end up on the table of enslaved people? Perhaps high-status tea wares in this context can be explained by the common practice of passing down dishware from the enslaver because the pot was damaged or no longer in stye. Any of these scenarios could explain the presence of these teapots as Scott was affluent and had access to expensive wares from Annapolis. But, the enslaver was not the sole route that tea wares reached the Belvoir Quarter. Indeed, refined wares such as these could be bought or traded by enslaved people.

The community who occupied the quarter after 1814 also drank teas and coffee held in whiteware pots either painted with flowers applied in broad brushstrokes or wrapped in blue transfer-prints. In addition, they used Rockingham teapots that resembled the brown "cat's eye" color as well as basic yellowware pots. By the mid-19th century, the enslaved household poured hot beverages from robust thick-bodied white ceramic pots known as graniteware. The variety of teapots and tea wares speaks to the regular and continued consumption of teas and other beverages steeped in pots from the 18th through the mid-19th centuries (Figure 4.7). The absence of porcelain tea pots and few high-status wares in general reflects not only an enslaved occupation but a middling estate, particularly by the early 19th century, a marked economic shift from Scott's tenure.

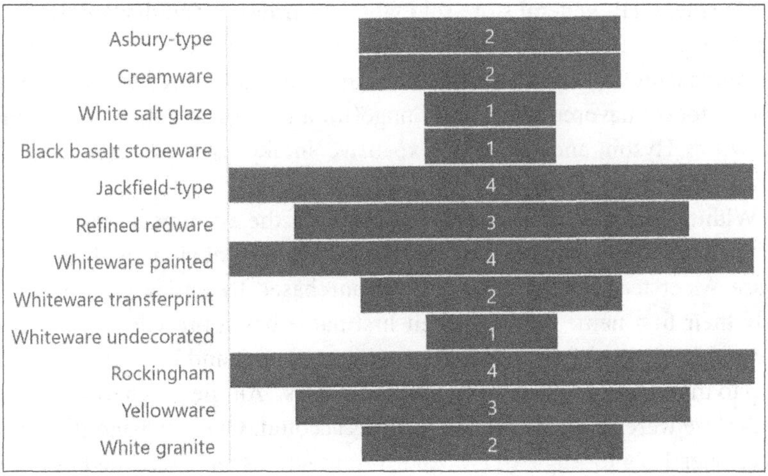

Figure 4.7. Distribution of tea ware types by number over time from oldest to most recent. (Courtesy of the Maryland Department of Transportation.)

British potteries produced ceramic pieces to accommodate European dining styles with each form serving a specific function. While adults and children drank tea and coffee, few studies have considered participation in this ritual by enslaved African Americans (Williams 1996:126). While we commonly find tea ware in these contexts, we are cautioned against assuming their use of ceramics was the same as the enslaver. While teacups in enslaved domestic contexts can mean awareness of the elite ritual, it does not equate to compliance or imitation of the formal tea service (Singleton 1995:127; Galle 2010:26). Indeed, the absence of societal boundaries surrounding the tea culture for these households meant flexibility in their use of cups; saucers were unnecessary, and the hollow form could be used to scoop and hold all types of liquids. Although a formal tea service ceremony may not have played out within the walls of a quarter, enslaved people still drank tea and, at a minimum, used teacups and mugs to sip warm beverages. They regularly treated illnesses with herbs, salves, and teas. Herbal teas made from mint, life everlasting, and wood betony, for example, were drunk in times of sickness (FWP 1941:18,50; Perdue et al. 1976:201; Wilkie 1996:122).

A close study of historic store ledgers in Virginia revealed enslaved African Americans purchasing tea and tea sets. Interestingly, while several varieties of black and green tea were available, most of the enslaved consumers appeared to gravitate toward light green teas called Hyson and Imperial (Greer 2020). This study inspired me to find merchant ledgers in Annapolis to determine whether enslaved people living near Belvoir also purchased tea and whether they preferred green teas over black teas. John Davidson was a late 18th-century merchant who kept a book of transactions for his Annapolis business. His general store sold fabrics, hardware, and dry goods. Looking through the years 1784 and 1785, I found over one dozen entries of people purchasing tea from Davidson. The merchant sold three teas during this time: a toasty flavored black tea, Congo(u); a green tea with an earthy taste known as Hyson; and the more expensive smoky-flavored black tea called Bohea (Davidson Day Book 1774–1775).

Within Davidson's ledger was the name of the account holder followed by the name of the person who charged to the account along with their purchase. Most teas appear to have been purchased by enslaved people, with only their first name listed, or their first name being preceded by the word "negro." White and free customers were given a first and last name, relationship to the account holder, or preceded by "Mrs." All the purchases at Davidson's store were charged to a free person's account. Over an 8-month period, December 1774 to August 1775, 20 tea transactions were recorded in Davidson's daybook, and 18 were purchased by enslaved African Americans. Out of these, eight orders of Hyson tea, seven orders of Congou, and three orders of Bohea tea were charged against store accounts. In three of the transactions, both Hyson and Congou tea were purchased in equal quantities. One entry by Scott was found in Davidson's 1782 ledger and documents his purchase of Soushong tea. This is a black tea similar to Congou tea with a smoky pine flavor. Based on these findings, it is impossible to determine a preference among the enslaved community in Annapolis. Furthermore, it is possible the entries reflect purchases by the enslaved for the enslaver's family, and, therefore, store ledgers may not always reveal individual or community preferences. At a minimum the analysis demonstrates which teas were available and that Bohea tea was the least consumed variety, perhaps due to a strong flavor and higher cost.

UTILITARIAN WARES

Since the front half of the stone quarter served as a large kitchen, we expected to find artifacts related to food preparation and storage. Chunky fragments of stoneware and thinner-bodied yellowware were found within and outside of the building. Yellowware was a common, everyday ceramic first imported into the American colonies during the 18th century from Scotland and England (Gallo 1985:10). Continuing in popularity throughout the years, these wares peaked during the mid-19th century, especially in Maryland. In Baltimore, the Edwin Bennett Pottery Company produced yellowware beginning in 1846, continuing through the 1930s (Leibowitz 1985:9,16). These food preparation bowls, pans, and plates were made from a yellow-colored clay fired with a clear glaze, allowing the yellow color of the paste to show. Sometimes hollowware pieces were decorated with a raised beaded relief around the exterior or painted with concentric bands of brown, blue, and/or white colors. In the Belvoir Quarter, we recovered 85 yellowware sherds that primarily represented mixing and batter bowls as well as a strainer; some are decorated. A few flatware pieces collected from the site included milk pans and pie plates.

Another common food preparation and storage ceramic type shipped in from England and created locally was coarse- and fine-grained redwares. Across North America, potters collected red clays from river and creek banks, set up a local kiln, and produced everything from cups to chamber pots. Indeed, Indigenous people had been creating their own clay pots from the same Maryland soil hundreds of years earlier. Made without shell or gravel temper like Native pottery, these redwares were fired at a higher temperature and could be coarse or finer bodied. Some were decorated with straight and wavy bands of white or yellow slip, while other vessels remained undecorated. The coarse redwares at Belvoir were related to food making and baking. Most of the fragments belonged to plates or platters that could have been used for pies or loaf dishes. We also found sherds from milk pans and bowls as well as a porringer.

The variety and number of artifacts associated with food preparation and storage demonstrate the importance of these containers to enslaved households. Local potters often bartered for goods they needed, and enslaved people would have easily fit into this commodity exchange, thereby facilitating their acquisition of redwares (Haskin 1941:180; Schablitsky 2007:42). When Bloch and Agbe-Davies (2017:124–125) looked closely at the use of food storage containers by enslaved people in the Chesapeake region, they noticed utilitarian ceramics decreased in use over time while the number of tablewares increased. Initially, this overall pattern appeared to be related to the increased access to finer ceramics from England and the replacement of the low-fired redwares with glass and metal containers. When the location on the plantation was considered, however, they learned the enslaved field laborers' use of utilitarian vessels remained constant while those working closer with the enslaver's family (domestic and skilled workers) declined. In other words, enslaved households responsible for storing and preparing meals required more utilitarian wares than did enslaved workers benefiting from a centralized food source.

After the Civil War, industrial potteries were also responsible for the replacement of local redwares almost exclusively with stoneware (Guilland 1971). Stoneware is a highly vitrified ceramic type commonly finished through salt glazing and sold or traded by potters primarily as a utilitarian ware. In Maryland, British-made stoneware arrived in the early 18th century with about half a dozen potters springing up in Virginia soon thereafter (Hunter and Goodman 2005:37). As with redwares, enslaved households commonly invested in the purchase and acquisition of these containers as they kept food moist, slowed evaporation of liquids, and reduced insect infestations (Bloch and Agbe-Davies 2017:127). The most common vessel forms used for food preparation and storage within kitchens included churns, jugs, jars, and vessels (Greer 1981).

Stoneware is a higher-fired clay and thicker bodied, so it survives in relatively large pieces on archaeological sites. The largest ceramic fragments at Belvoir came from stoneware crocks decorated with splashes of cobalt-blue glaze (Figure 4.8). We collected many of these fragments in the yard space outside of the kitchen. Specifically, we recovered 72 stoneware sherds, most of the fragments (47 sherds) were gray with only 16 tan stoneware sherds and 1 interior and exterior white-glazed stoneware milk pan (9 sherds). Even a small stoneware pie weight was found within the home. The tan stoneware sherds represent a bowl and jug. The more numerous gray stoneware included a variety of vessels including jars, bowls, pitchers, jugs, and a butter churn (Figure 4.9). Another interesting coarse earthenware piece we recovered from this site was a pipkin handle. Pipkins are pots with a hollow handle used to heat food over coals and near indirect flames.

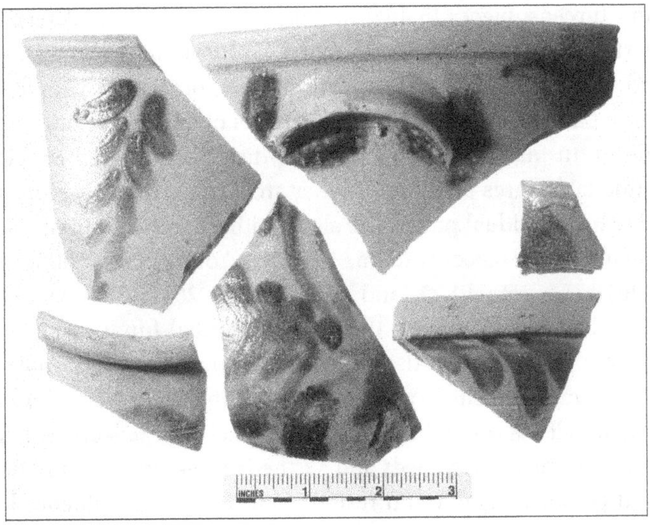

Figure 4.8. Stoneware crock fragments with cobalt-blue glaze dating to the first half of the 19th century. (Courtesy of the Maryland Department of Transportation.)

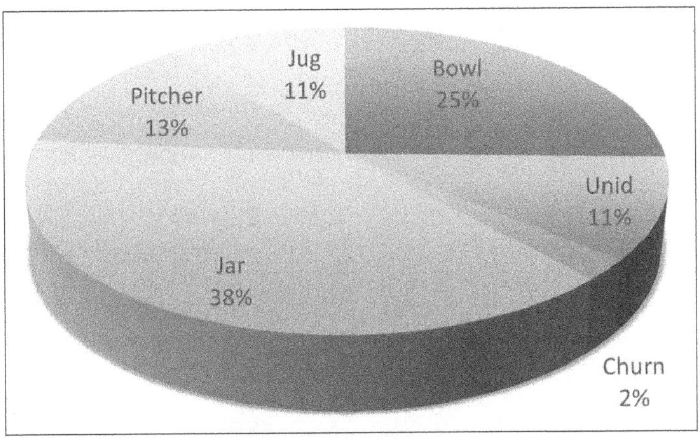

Figure 4.9. Percentage of gray stoneware vessel forms associated with Belvoir Quarter. Unid = unidentified. (Courtesy of the Maryland Department of Transportation.)

When reflecting upon the Belvoir Quarter's large ceramic assemblage, it seems contradictory to find delicate, floral-decorated cups and saucers within a context of human brutality. It is unlikely, however, this fragile ceramic collection matched the quality and forms used inside of the manor home. We found few porcelain or other high-end ceramics and an absence of covered bowls and tureens, pieces that commonly accompany formal sets. The Belvoir Quarter artifact catalog listed a few sugar bowls and creamers. Although we found numerous cups printed with flowers, birds, and people, only the Caledonian pattern may have belonged to a set of dishes. We often attribute a collection of mismatched and inexpensive dishes to enslaved people acquiring ceramic tablewares piecemeal. Other archaeologists suggest mismatched pieces may be individual preference along with a combination of trading and recycling of ceramic pieces (Mullins 1999:150; Young 2004; Wilkie and Farnsworth 2010:156–159; Bloch and Agbe-Davies 2017:135). Although mismatched dishes may have been the result of limited funds or access for enslaved people, it could have also been an opportunity to defy an established tableware norm and formality associated with their enslaver. Choosing each piece individually and combining them in a set that reflected the enslaved community's meal service needs and aesthetic preferences would have communicated personal agency and resistance to European-influenced customs and behavior.

5
Consuming and Supplementing

> It sometimes happened, too, in the lower counties of Maryland, that there was an allowance of pork, made to the slaves one day in each week; If they chose to fish, they had the privilege of selling whatever they caught.
>
> —Charles Ball (1859:43), formerly enslaved Marylander

In the Chesapeake region, planters commonly provided the enslaved community with a ration of maize supplemented with occasional cuts of beef and mutton from the animals' lower limbs, heads, and feet (Breeden 1980:90). Many formerly enslaved people claimed their food was both insufficient and lacking in variety (Henson 1849:6; Ball 1859:11–12). Abolitionist Frederick Douglass (1845:10), born enslaved on the Eastern Shore of Maryland, reported they were only given eight pounds of pork and/or fish a month along with one bushel of cornmeal. The formerly enslaved Marylander Charles Ball (1859:17) recalled, "We had a tolerable supply of meat for a short time, about the month of December, when he killed his hogs. After that season we had meat once a week, unless bacon became scarce, which very often happened, in which case we had no meat at all. However, as we fortunately lived near both the Patuxent river and the Chesapeake Bay, we had abundance of fish in the spring, and as long as the fishing season continued. After that period, each slave received, in addition to his allowance of corn, one salt herring every day."

One difference in opinion among enslavers was whether to dole out rations of whole food at the beginning of the week or to prepare two meals a day. Although it was much easier to pass out a week's worth of meat and grain, the enslaved households would then be responsible for processing and preparing the food. The enslavers believed this method of food distribution impacted time for rest and encouraged trading away weekly rations for other items. To discourage this behavior, they often directed an enslaved cook to prepare two meals a day. Enslavers believed this arrangement ensured the food was processed and cooked properly, thereby improving palatability and avoiding food-borne illnesses (Breeden 1980:20). Sometimes the method used to distribute food depended on the location and composition of the household. Individual family units located a distance from the manor home may have been given rations to prepare, while those living closer to the main estate may have eaten food prepared by a more centrally located enslaved cook (Neiman 2008:176–178). The Belvoir Quarter had a large kitchen where a cook prepared meals for enslaved people living inside and immediately adjacent to the manor home. Many of the meals likely reflected West African cooking styles using a single pot to simmer stews and soups (Franklin 2001:97). Although recipes and detailed discussions on African diaspora foodways are not discussed here, I acknowledge that enslaved communities prepared meals that maintained their culture and identity. As cooks adapted to their new environment and culture, the substitution of African ingredients for locally available food resulted in creolized dishes. Franklin (2015:135) explains that the preservation of these traditional foods maintained African culture as well as bonded groups and encouraged social interactions between communities.

FAUNAL REMAINS

One of the most important datasets on an archaeology site are faunal remains left behind from the processing and consumption of domestic and wild-caught meat. The diagnostic attributes of each bone can tell faunal analysts the species and age of an animal when butchered. They also look at cut marks to determine, for example, whether the meat was taken off the bone with a knife or chopped into smaller pieces for a stew. A calcined bone that shows "pot polish" is evidence of boiling for a broth, while a blackened bone fragment suggests roasted meat. The cut of meat can also provide information about people's economic status on a plantation. If a large part of the faunal assemblage represents meaty, flavorful, and desired cuts of meat such as beef tenderloin, we surmise higher class status. In contrast, a significant number of jaw fragments and limb bones, insinuating the incorporation of lower and less valuable pieces of the animal into the diet, suggests a poverty diet.

Many archaeologists studying sites of enslavement, regardless of region, often find enslaved households consistently consumed pork, much less beef, primarily less meaty cuts of domesticated older animals, and a healthy number of fish and wild fauna. In Virginia, at Flowerdew Hundred, a quarter site contained an 1830s feature with a variety of animal bones with high numbers of pork and catfish but very few beef and sheep bones; even chicken was consumed more often than beef (McKee 1999:228–230). At Andrew Jackson's Hermitage Estate, pork was the most consumed domestic animal; beef and sheep were found in much lower numbers. Additionally, all the domestic cuts of meat, regardless of species, represented less meaty and lower limbs of the animal (Thomas 1998:543). While pork and lower cuts of meat are common on many of these sites, other studies show a more complex and varied subsistence pattern among enslaved households (Crader 1990:691; Fennell 2011:13). Challenging the generalization of these diets is a study on the faunal remains from Thomas Jefferson's enslaved community. When archaeologists compared their data against the findings from other enslaved households, they saw unexpected differences. While pork still dominated, there seemed to be a higher prevalence of beef and better cuts of meat at one of Jefferson's enslaved homes referred to as Building "o." Crader (1990:713) surmised either food remains from the mansion became comingled with the enslaved households food or they truly were eating better food.

Dozens of people living in the Belvoir Quarter for about 80 years produced over 22,000 faunal remains representing domestic and wild-caught animals. On average, the estate supported a population of several enslaved adults assigned to the central manor home as well as about one dozen enslaved field laborers. While an enslaved cook prepared and fed the Belvoir Quarter's household, they also packed and transported meals around the estate, including the fields. Anything with bone, particularly chicken and fish, would have been carried elsewhere and deposited away from the quarter kitchen. Although never identified archaeologically, Belvoir manor likely had a closer and separate kitchen up the hill, where an enslaved cook prepared meals for the planter family and their guests. The enslaved domestic workers had access to this food, including any uneaten plated food cleared from the table (Ball 1859:206; Franklin 2019:121). Cuts of meat from the manor home could easily be carried down to the Belvoir Quarter to be eaten and thrown away. As bone from these meals would be incidental inclusions, I did not expect expensive or meaty cuts to dominate this faunal assemblage.

We studied 11 archaeological features with over 10,000 specimens associated with the Belvoir Quarter, and most of the bone came from kitchen features and the subfloor pit (Crowl et al. 2022:Appendix D). Ralph Koziarski analyzed faunal material from this site, including remains found outside the home and across other parts of the yard, but these bone fragments were not incorporated into this analysis since they were not associated with a tightly dated feature and had few diagnostic elements. The Belvoir Quarter faunal assemblage consisted of wild, domestic, and maritime animals (Figure 5.1). There were many oysters and a smaller number of clams throughout the site and across time. We also noted small rodents, but as none of them appeared to have been processed for food, they are not discussed here and were likely opportunistic visitors in the home.

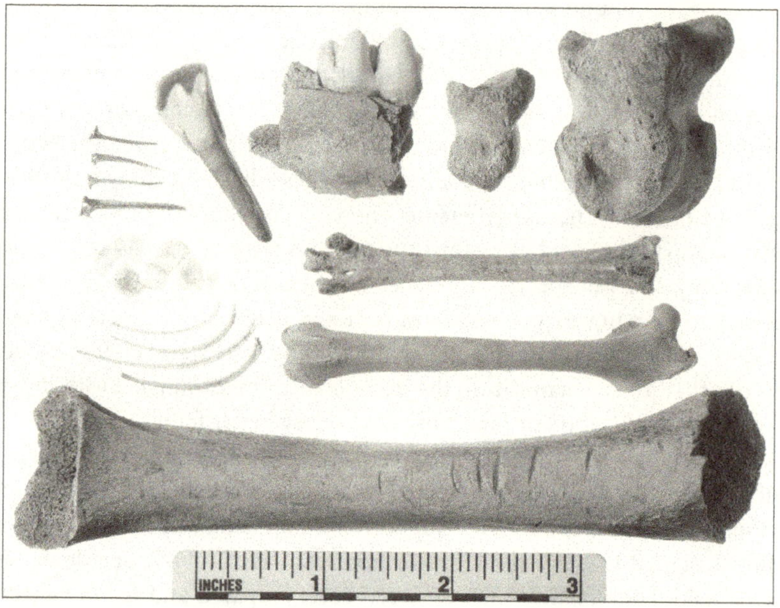

Figure 5.1. *Top row* (*left to right*), fish vertebrae, pig incisor, cow mandible, pig phalanx, cow phalanx. *Middle row* (*left to right*), bass fish scales and fish ribs, chicken metatarsal, and eastern cottontail femur. *Bottom*, sheep/goat radius with cut marks. (Courtesy of the Maryland Department of Transportation.)

DOMESTIC MAMMALS

The domestic mammals eaten by Belvoir's enslaved people included cattle, pigs, and sheep/goats. In the spring of 1816, while processing the estate of his late uncle, Scott, and liquidating his own possessions from Belvoir, Maynadier sold merino and common sheep. Most were ewes or lambs (*MG* 1816). Despite the herds of sheep at Belvoir, the enslaved household consumed very little mutton. They did, however, butcher a healthy number of rabbits including domesticated European hare. As expected, Belvoir's enslaved community relied heavily on pork, and it was usually in the form of heads, feet, and limbs (Crowl et al. 2022:Appendix D). While not a regular event, they also butchered entire hogs and likely received rations of pork fat. Pigs were an easy food source since they were meaty, inexpensive, and could be raised anywhere (Yentsch 1994:230; Walsh et al. 1997:84; Franklin 2004:190).

Belvoir's enslaved community also ate beef, albeit less frequently than pork, but much more often than mutton. All animal bones, including those with tougher meat from the lower limbs of cattle, can be rendered into broths, soups, and stews to feed numerous people at once. In addition, most cultures, including those from Africa, have recipes for stewed beef cheek

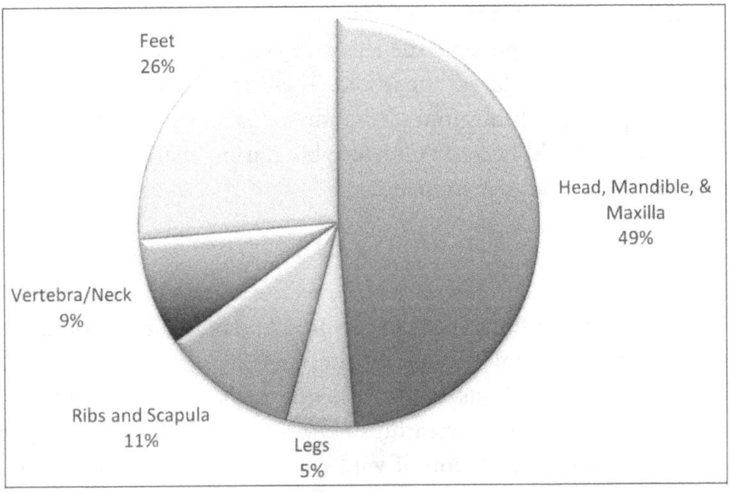

Figure 5.2. Percentage of beef cuts found at the Belvoir Quarter. (Courtesy of the Maryland Department of Transportation.)

meat and calves foot jelly. Scott bred black cattle and sheep at Belvoir and exported barrels of salted beef to the U.S. military (Howard Papers 1662–1919; Selig 2015:21,67). Salted beef packed in barrels only includes the meaty portions while the heads and lower limbs of the cattle are usually left out (English 1990; Brophy and Crisman 2013:71–72). When they butchered cattle at Belvoir, the enslaver likely kept the better cuts of meat for themselves. Considering Belvoir's beef export business through the early 19th century, along with the expense of keeping cattle, any beef distributed to the enslaved community likely included heads, lower limbs, and feet. They may have also been provided with offal, an archaeologically invisible ration. Unsurprisingly, we find the opposite faunal pattern when enslaved households only have access to salted beef. At a Caribbean sugar plantation in Martinique, archaeologists found the enslaved households ate beef from the axial and limb elements with very few cranial and foot remains represented (Handler and Wallman 2014:455). The cut marks on the faunal remains, along with reliance of cattle in Martinique as draft animals, suggested the beef arrived cured in barrels. In this case, the heads and feet of the cattle were left behind at the butchery.

Studying the faunal catalog listing the domestic cuts of meat within and immediately surrounding the Belvoir Quarter, I noted that 75% of the beef bone represented feet and heads, even after excluding loose teeth. The remaining beef cuts included low numbers of lower limbs, ribs, a scapula, a neck bone, and vertebrae (Figure 5.2). Since the export of cattle from Belvoir only continued through the War of 1812, this only partially explains the low number of beef limbs. It is possible the legs and even some feet may have been provided to another enslaved household. These numbers may also be low if the cook chopped the limbs into pieces for soups and stews. The small beef bone fragments would become undetectable during analysis and only cataloged as medium to large mammal.

WILD FAUNA

While investing time and resources into wild-caught game may have been necessary to stave off hunger, inclusion into enslaved diets should also be considered an individual choice and preference (Franklin 2001:99). Both enslaver and enslaved households enjoyed the taste of maritime foods, ducks, and other woodland creatures (Lev-Tov 1998). It is also important to consider their incorporation of wild-caught meat into traditional African dishes (Franklin 2001; Scott 2001:687). As Belvoir was near Annapolis and along the Severn River and Round Bay, the enslaved community enjoyed a diet rich in fish, crab, and oysters. Additionally, they may have regularly set snares to capture raccoons, opossum, and rabbits to secure food but also to sell or trade their pelts (Ball 1859:195–196). In the woodlands and around home, they could gather turtles and snakes while going about their work. What we would not expect to see in the faunal assemblage at Belvoir, however, is a significant number of animals requiring longer periods of hunting with firearms, such as deer. Firearms may have been in limited supply and only allowed to be carried by certain enslaved people. Furthermore, hunting took time away from other duties around the estate. Although lengthy hunting trips may not have been common among enslaved people, they were entrusted with firearms for hunting and regularly brought down a variety of birds including ducks, geese, and turkey (Morgan 1998:139). In the Belvoir Quarter, we found 10 gray-and-tan colored gunflints within and around the building (Figure 5.3). Although most flints appeared to have been repurposed into "strike-a-lights" to create a spark for cooking and warming fires, there were three that had only been used in flintlock guns. Our recovery of a lead flint wrap confirmed enslaved people at Belvoir used flintlock guns for hunting. Although lead shot can be hard to find because it slips through quarter-inch mesh screens during an archaeological excavation, we collected soil samples from the features and found several "bird shot" and a .45-caliber lead ball inside the home. The shot likely came from cleaning and eating birds and other wild game. It is unlikely Belvoir's enslaved household stored any significant amount of munitions in the quarter.

Figure 5.3. Gunflints (*top*), lead flint wrap (*bottom left*), and lead shot (*bottom center and right*). The gunflints could have been repurposed as strike-a-lights to spark a fire. (Courtesy of the Maryland Department of Transportation.)

CHICKENS

Chickens figured prominently in the lives of enslaved households as both egg bearers and a food source. Chickens and eggs could also be sold and traded. Despite the risk of being caught, enslaved people often became hungry enough to take fowl, hogs, and sheep from their own, or neighboring, estates (Morgan 1998:136). Usually, these incidents took place under the cover of night and any evidence of the carcass was buried, burned, or thrown in a river (Henson 1849:9; Perdue et al. 1976:244–245,266–267). Chickens were the most common animals taken; they were abundant, easily snagged, and could be quickly quieted. One of Booker T. Washington's (1901:5) earliest memories was of his mother cooking a chicken late at night and then waking him up to feed him. To hide the evidence, they burned the feathers (Savitt 2002:97). A formerly enslaved man in Virginia recalled being so desperate he grabbed chickens right off the roost. Taking them at night, they hid the chickens in a pit with a trapdoor (Perdue et al. 1976:116).

FIREPLACES AND KITCHEN SUBFLOOR PIT

Although we recovered animal bones outside of and inside of the home across many features, the kitchen's root cellar or subfloor pit held a high number of animal bones from the first half of the 19th century. As mentioned, subfloor pits were common in homes of enslaved people, and once they began to fail at food storage, the pits transformed into refuse pits filled with household waste. At Monticello, at least six of the households enslaved by Jefferson eventually used their root cellar as a pit to throw away a variety of artifacts and animal bones (Crader 1990:710–711). At the Belvoir Quarter, we segregated the soil from the subfloor pit into two different contexts based on soil morphology: Feature 47 and Feature 49 (Figure 5.4). A lens of soil adjacent to the west wall of the subfloor pit (Feature 39) contained late 18th- and early 19th-century artifacts and appears to have been created when the hand-dug cellar was cleaned out. The first community to live in the quarter and use the small cellar for food storage was the household enslaved by the Scott family. When their subfloor pit failed, they filled the collapsed pit with wild-caught and domestic animal bones as well as other household artifacts such as buttons and ceramic sherds dating to the late 18th and early 19th centuries (Feature 49).

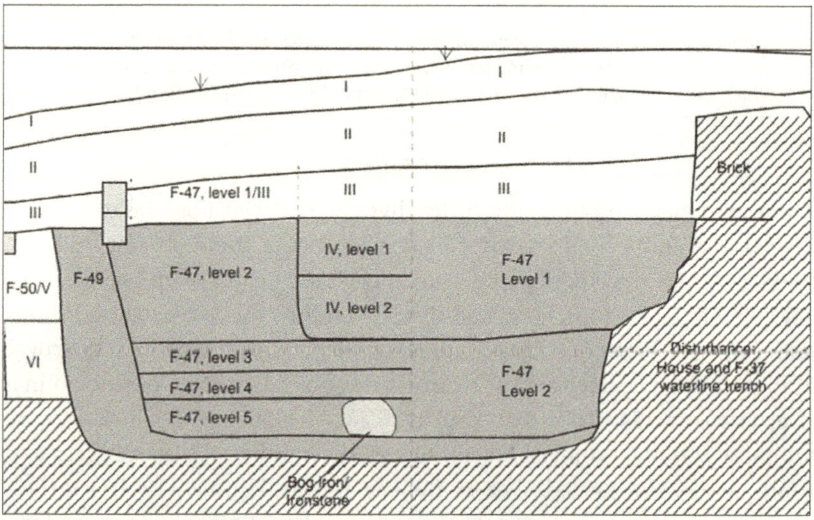

Figure 5.4. Excavation units 53 and 55 with north wall profile of Features 47 (F-47) and 49 (F-49). The subfloor pit soils are dark gray. The soil levels were excavated and screened separately. Feature 39 (not pictured) was adjacent to the west (left) side of the feature. (Courtesy of the Maryland Department of Transportation.)

We collected over 1,300 bones and fish scales from Features 39 and 49 by dry and wet screening the soil through 1/8-in. screens. The number of bones appears relatively high in number, but it is skewed from numerous fish bones and scales. The maritime animals and fish included drum, bowfin, perch, bass, catfish, herring, sunfish, and trout with blue crab, mussels, and oysters. Wild-caught animals included turkey, rabbit, and squirrel/chipmunk. Domestic animals were primarily represented by the distal limbs and head elements from pig; a scapula, thoracic vertebrae, and lower limbs from a cow; along with chickens and eggshells.

When the household enslaved by the Worthingtons moved into the quarter around 1816, they excavated the backfilled subfloor pit and filled it with their own kitchen refuse at least twice before it was abandoned in the 1840s (Feature 47). We recovered 6,000 animal bones from the pit, including oyster and mussel shells. The wild-caught animals netted and snared for food included a fair number of squirrels, turtles, and rabbits, with smaller numbers of frog, snake, and racoon elements. The fish caught and eaten were similar to those found in Features 39 and 49 and represented approximately half of the faunal remains. Domestic animals included cows, sheep/goats, pigs, and rabbits. Most of the medium to large mammal bones came from the animals' legs, feet, and heads.

The faunal remains contributed by the household enslaved by the Welsh family could only be isolated to the back bedroom fireplaces. The northwest bedroom, without access to the kitchen, held several animal bones around and within the hearth. The domestic faunal material came from chickens, pigs, and sheep/goats while the wild-caught fauna included an eastern gray squirrel and rabbit. Only the left tibia of a domestic rabbit was found in the northeast room's fireplace. It is intriguing to consider Belvoir's enslaved community raising not only chickens but also rabbits as food sources. The northeast bedroom was likely the cook's quarters, and she had direct access to the kitchen, so the bedroom hearth was less likely to be used to prepare meals.

We had intact archaeological deposits, so it was possible to compare and contrast the similarities and differences between the first two enslaved households. As mentioned, pork followed by beef was the most consumed animal (Crowl et al. 2022:Appendix D). The same pattern emerged when I looked at the distribution of cuts between the households enslaved by the Worthingtons and the Scotts. But, when we looked at the minimum number of individual animals consumed by faunal class (e.g., mammal, fish, bird), the distributions between these two enslaved households changed. The household enslaved by the Scotts relied heavily on mammals and fish as well as crabs (Figure 5.5), while the household enslaved by the Worthingtons consumed more birds, sheep/goats. They also added turtles, snakes, and frogs to their diet (Figure 5.6). The addition of amphibians and reptiles to their diet, as well as a fox or dog, owl, and a perching bird, suggests the community enslaved by the Worthingtons had less domestic meat and relied more heavily on woodland creatures. Specifically, they consumed 6% more wild mammals than the household enslaved by the Scotts (Crowl et al. 2022:Appendix D).

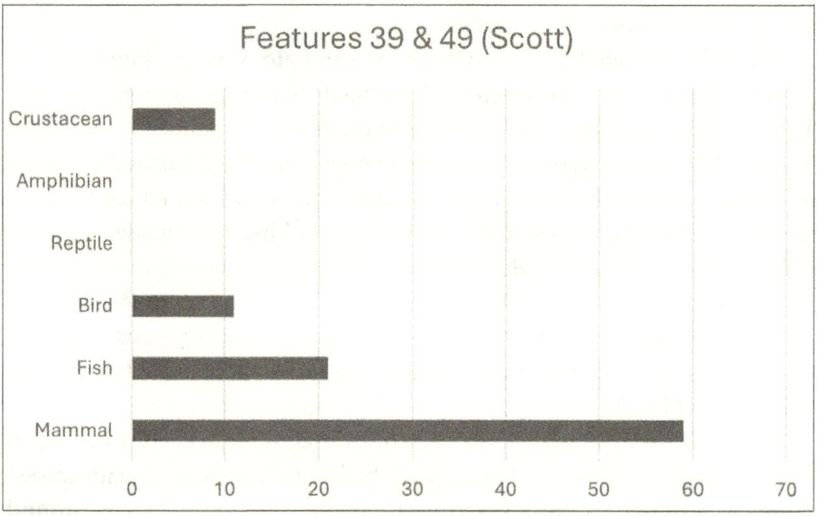

Figure 5.5. Distribution of the number of identified faunal bones by animal class found in Features 39 and 49 in household enslaved by the Scotts. (Courtesy of the Maryland Department of Transportation.)

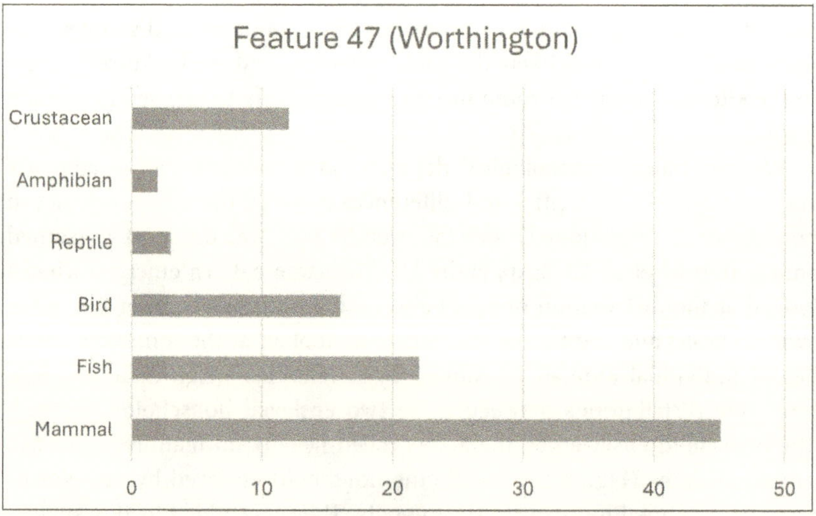

Figure 5.6. Distribution of number of identified faunal bones by animal class found in Feature 47 of the household enslaved by the Worthingtons. Reptiles and amphibians appear in their diet. (Courtesy of the Maryland Department of Transportation.)

BOTANICAL REMAINS

In addition to meat, the enslaved household grew, harvested, and ate grains, vegetables, and fruit. Usually, small garden plots were located near the home where they could easily maintain the plantings on breaks, Sundays, or in the evening, often working by moonlight (FWP 1941; Heath and Bennett 2000:41). These small garden plots, referred to as a "truck patch" by Josiah Henson (1849:7), grew a variety of plants used for food, medicine, and utilitarian purposes. Enslaved people were given very little space, so being able to prepare soil to grow vegetables and raise animals allowed them opportunities to express their skills in horticulture and animal husbandry. Just as importantly, it demonstrated self-reliance. One woman enslaved in Virginia recalled that gardens were common, and everyone grew gourds on vines to be used as dippers (Perdue et al. 1976:16). Ball (1859:12) recalled his father bringing him apples, melons, or sweet potatoes when he visited. These foods grew in nearby gardens, orchards, adjacent woodlands, and fields. Both men and women participated in the maintenance and harvesting of fruits and vegetables. Some enslaved people also managed a garden to earn money or trade for things they, family, or friends might need or desire. Ball (1859:130) remembered the storekeepers as eager to engage with enslaved people because they did not require credit and could demand unfair prices without a care of being held accountable.

We commonly take soil samples from subsurface features such as pits, hearths, or other dark soil-stained areas because there is a high potential for charred organic artifacts. At Belvoir we collected dozens of soil samples in hopes of recovering carbonized wood and grains, as well as seeds, shells, and pits from fruits, vegetables, grains, and nuts. When organics are carbonized (burned), they are temporarily stabilized if the microenvironment they are buried within is stable. Soil samples can also capture fish bones and scales, straight pins, beads, and other tiny artifacts. Archaeologists working at the Rich Neck Slave Quarter in Virginia took soil samples to reconstruct the historic landscape and to understand what the enslaved community consumed beyond meat (Franklin 2004). They recovered many honey locust seeds, showing the heavy use of this plant as a sweetener and tea. When the archaeobotanist looked closely at the other carbonized remains, they recognized a variety of garden vegetables including peanuts, melons, squash, beans, and black-eyed peas. Grains such as corn, rye, barley, and wheat were also recovered by these archaeologists (Franklin 2004:175–177). Monticello's enslaved community ate grains such as maize, wheat, oats, rye, and sorghum. Fruits and nuts from this site included peaches, strawberry, raspberry, elderberry, grapes, sumac, hickory, and walnut. (Bowes and Trigg 2012:161–164).

The preservation and successful recovery of charred seeds from the Belvoir Quarter allowed us to partially reconstruct the plant diet of the enslaved household. To capture the last meals prepared in the stone quarter, we collected dark-colored soils from inside and near the kitchen fireplace and the two corner fireplaces. As we found numerous domestic artifacts related to food preparation and consumption on the west side of the building, we also collected soil here. At the laboratory, an archaeobotanist poured the soil into water where it was agitated to loosen any charred wood, seeds, or pits. They poured the organic slurry through small sieves. After the sample dried, the archaeologist picked the carbonized organics out, placed them under a microscope, and identified the charred botanical artifacts.

The Belvoir Quarter's central fireplace was destroyed decades earlier when a cinderblock basement was installed for a small wood building that incorporated part of the historic stone foundation. Despite the disturbance, dark stains survived around one of the remaining stones that once formed the kitchen hearth. We learned the kitchen fireplace burned a variety of wood including pine, chestnut, and some oak. Charred bits of maize revealed the enslaved household ground and processed corn here. We also found evidence of cherries, grapes, and black walnuts. The archaeobotanist also identified charred seeds from wheat and oat or rye—evidence of grains in their diet (Crowl et al. 2022:Appendix E).

One of the more curious discoveries we made from the northwest corner fireplace was bulrush seeds. In this context, bulrush could have been used as a food source, for baskets, or bedding. If used for food, the seeds would have been ground into flour to make bread or boiled into a mush. The soft flower that contained the seeds may have been used as soft stuffing in pillows and beds while the reeds could have been woven into mats and baskets. Based on historic accounts, enslaved Africans wove bulrush reeds into baskets (Johnson et al. 2008; Crowl et al. 2022:Appendix E). There are even reports of rush mats being used as beds (Morgan 1998:114). When Ball (1859:113–114) visited a cabin where enslaved people lived, he stated it had very little furniture with "a small bed in one corner, composed of a mat, made of common rushes, spread upon some corn husks, pulled and split into fine pieces, and kept together by a narrow slip of wood, confined to the floor by wooden pins."

For years, a 20th-century single-story building sat on top of much of the original stone quarter. As such, preservation was very good, particularly in the northeast corner bedroom where the entire base of the corner hearth survived. It was so intact that charcoal from the last fire still clung to the soft red bricks. I gathered the dark soil within this hearth as well as from the remains of the northwest corner fireplace. Careful collection of the soil in the northeast hearth, possibly where the cook and her family slept, showed this fireplace was indeed used for cooking up until it was abandoned. Archaeobotanist Kathleen Furgerson carried out flotation analysis and water screened this soil. She recovered an unidentified nutshell, oat and wheat seeds, as well as bits of squash rind (Crowl et al. 2022:Appendix E). Food was being processed and consumed not only in the kitchen but also in this space, at least during the mid-19th century. The squash rind was an interesting discovery as archaeologists seldom find evidence of gourd dippers or bowls. Although the flesh of the squash could have been eaten, it is likely the rind would have been fashioned into something practical like a dipper. The presence of violet seeds was initially curious as well but would be appropriate in this context. The flowers are edible and can be used as a medicinal herb for coughing and as an anti-inflammatory (Blankespoor 2018). We also took a soil sample from around the hearth in the northwest room. The bricks were badly damaged and only the bottom of the hearth and front area survived modern construction. Regardless, the soil sample contained possible wheat chaffs and fig seeds. The presence of wheat and figs in this room supports use as a place to both prepare and consume food.

Both the faunal and macrobotanical analysis revealed an amazing amount of data on the diet of Belvoir's enslaved community. Archaeological remains of carbonized grains, seeds, and even a squash rind showed the enslaved households incorporated locally grown food into their diets. Based on oral histories and the archaeology from other similar sites, a garden to grow food was tended by the enslaved households and likely significantly contributed to their diet and perhaps created an avenue of revenue for them. While the collection of carbonized seeds and pits can provide a list of the types of plants they grew and ate, close analysis of the faunal remains is where we can better understand the health and nutrition of enslaved people and dietary changes between households.

Because we were studying a place where people were deprived of human rights, I expected to see expressions of suffering and starvation in the form of low cuts of meat from older animals and a high number of wild-caught animals. I predicted the enslaved community would receive small rations, and a representative sample of old animals past their prime. If a cow was to be butchered for meat, for example, the more flavorful and tender cuts would have been prepared for the enslaver or exported for a profit, while the lower cuts of meat would have been distributed to the enslaved families. These are expected results, but I also wondered whether there were differences over time between the people enslaved by the Scotts, Worthingtons, and Welshes. Was one household provided additional or better food than another? Did the amount of wild fauna increase or decrease over time? If so, what does this tell us about how the enslaved people were treated and was the economic status of the enslaver a factor? After studying the faunal remains, as discussed, I concluded the quality of food, particularly domestic cuts of meat, did not drastically differ among Belvoir's enslaved households over time. Pork appeared to be a significant source of meat, particularly when considering the archaeologically invisible rations of bacon (Reitz 1987:114–115; Scott 2001:686). In addition, everyone added wild-caught food to their diet out of preference and necessity. The household enslaved by the Worthingtons, however, ate higher numbers and a wider variety of wild-caught animals with the addition of reptiles and amphibians.

I further wondered whether they ate enough food to keep hunger away. Was a diet of cornmeal, some domestic meat, woodland creatures, and garden vegetables nutritious enough to keep their bodies healthy enough to fight off sickness and disease? Bioarchaeologists can often recognize evidence of diseases, infections, and malnutrition in the bones and teeth of people, suggesting they suffered with pain and sickness while alive (Savitt 2002:89; Wilson and Cabak 2004:267, 276–279). In Southern Maryland, at the request of the African American Heritage Society of Charles County and descendant community, we studied the skeletal remains of 10 enslaved men, women, and children who died between 1790 and 1810 on the property of Henry Arundel Smith. One of the burials was a 25–34-year-old man with bowed legs who walked with a knock-kneed appearance. An insufficient amount of vitamin D during childhood caused him to suffer from rickets. Within the same burial ground, a 5–6-year-old child's front teeth showed indented lines. These severe enamel deformities formed during a period of nutritional distress during their life (Kollmann 2016:Appendix 10). Despite the apparent variety of food we found represented in the archaeological record, it is likely the enslaved community at Belvoir also struggled to meet their nutritional needs and suffered similarly.

6
Adorning and Signaling

> Henny, about twenty-five years of age, five feet, two or three inches high, with a very pleasant countenance when spoken to; had on, when she ran away, a short calico jacket, a black skirt, and a red striped handkerchief around her head; She was purchased of Doctor Scott, of Annapolis.
>
> —(*MG* 1805A)

The type of fabric and general design of an enslaved person's outfit accommodated their assignment in life but also reflected the expectations of the enslaver. Each year, they provided one set of clothing for warmer and cooler weather to include shoes, stockings, a hat, and a suit of clothes such as shirts, jackets and trousers for men, and petticoats and shifts for women (Ball 1859:17; Morgan 1998:125). The type of work enslaved men, women, and children performed dictated whether their clothing was made from strong, loosely fitting fabric to allow movement and air circulation, or tailored waistcoats and properly hemmed trousers. There was consensus among enslavers that good-quality fabric for bedding and clothing was important and should not be compromised. Oznabrig, similar to coarse linen, was commonly used for field laborers while fearnought, a heavy woolen fabric, clothed uniformed butlers and liverymen. The clothing for children was simple and loose fitting. Boys and girls under the age of seven wore dresses or frocks. After this time, the enslaved children dressed as adults and worked in the fields or around the estate (Baumgarten 1988:50). Leather shoes and boots may have been provided, but enslaved people also worked shoeless. At the Belvoir Quarter, we found dozens of metal fasteners, and most were basic D-shaped iron buckles that could have belonged to leather belts used on pants, bags, or animal harnesses (Figure 6.1). Buckles made from pewter or copper alloy adorned shoes and vests. Two copper alloy clothing buckles, likely worn by people enslaved by Thomas Welsh, had the year 1855 stamped on them. Enslaved men and women finished off their outfits with a head covering such as a felt hat or scarf (Morgan 1998:128–129). In 1790, Charles self-liberated from Brice Worthington's estate located next to Belvoir. He was reported taking two brown cloth and one fearnought jacket, a new country linen shirt, Welch cotton breeches, yarn stockings, shoes, and a felt hat (*MG* 1790). He likely wore basic leather shoes with minimum holes for laces. Shoes with buckles would have been more likely worn by those working in and around the manor home.

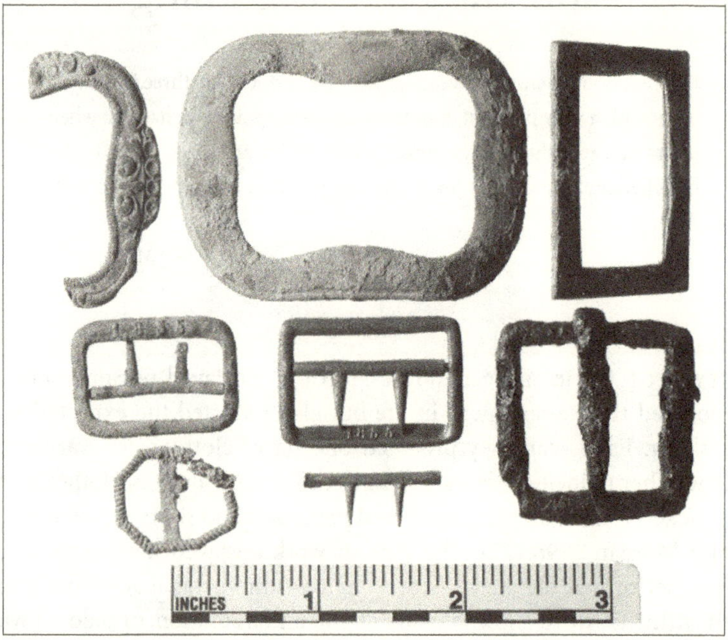

Figure 6.1. Shoe buckles (*top left and top center*), clothing buckles (*top far right, center left and middle, bottom far left and middle*), and leather belt/harness buckle (*bottom right*). (Courtesy of the Maryland Department of Transportation.)

Although planters supplied premade dresses, shirts, and pants, it was more economical to have their wives, daughters, or enslaved women make the clothing. Often, the cloth provided to enslaved women was precut to prevent the fabric from being traded or sold (Baumgarten 1988:42–43). Any worn or ripped clothing would have been patched and the stockings darned (Breeden 1980:140–141). In the Belvoir Quarter, we found dozens of straight pins, half a dozen thimbles, and a broken scissors for these tasks (Figure 6.2). Sometimes a pin would drop from their hands and become lost on the brick floor. Not surprisingly, we found most of the mending artifacts concentrated around the large fireplace in the kitchen, with a few straight pins and a thimble in the two back rooms, adjacent to the hearths. Articles of clothing could also be passed to enslaved people from the planter's family (Baumgarten 1988:39). Ball (1859:10) was given hand-me-down clothing from the enslaver's children. When clothing and fabric were provided to enslaved people to wear, they likely modified the garments to fit their individual body shapes and to reflect their own sense of style; they tucked loose cloth, strategically placed a stitch, and embellished their clothing with buttons, beads, and ribbons. While the type of uniform they wore was not in their control, enslaved people still used practical yet creative ways to express individuality, choice, and power through visual cues on their body.

Figure 6.2. Mending artifacts including thimbles, straight pins, and iron scissors. (Courtesy of the Maryland Department of Transportation.)

Anyone accompanying the planter's family into the city or serving within the manor home could have dressed in a three-piece suit (Baumgarten 1988:34–35). Caroline Hammond, a woman enslaved by Thomas Davidson, near Davidsonville in Anne Arundel County, recalled her family had certain privileges over others: "All of the cooking was supervised by mother, and the table was waited on by Uncle Billie, dressed in a uniform, decorated with brass buttons, braids and a fancy vest, his hands encased in white gloves" (FWP 1941:19). The type of cloth and the condition of an enslaved person's uniform were also related to the wealth of the enslaver and the message he wanted to publicly convey about his status (Thomas and Thomas 2004:114–115). Thomas Welsh, who purchased Belvoir in 1850, also owned a larger estate southwest of Annapolis at the head of South River. Basil, who was about 25 years old and around 5 ft. 11 in. tall, self-emancipated "wearing a ticklinburg [coarse linen] shirt, a roundabout jacket, and white kersey [coarse woolen] trousers, a striped linsey [linen and wool blend] under jacket, and newer stockings, coarse shoes, and an old white hat" (*MG* 1823). The formal outfit suggests he worked closely with the Welsh family. Basil was also mentioned as having "a pleasant countenance when spoken to," suggesting regular and close interaction with the Welsh family rather than someone who labored in the field. In the end, Basil was apprehended nine days later and held in the Frederick County jail, about 70 miles northwest of his home (*Daily National Intelligencer* 1823).

The enslaver assigned people to positions on his estate not only on skills and ability but also personality, verbal articulation, and physical appearance (Thomas and Thomas 2004:109). The planter's children born to enslaved women may have also found themselves in a creative arrangement within the manor home. Ball (1859:117) observed these conscious decisions, stating those who worked within the home were "chosen from the most handsome and sprightly of the gang." While their clothes and work duties, as well as the lightness of their skin, could influence how enslaved people were seen and treated by each other; they did not necessarily abide by this strict hierarchy (Thomas and Thomas 2004:109,116). It is probable the Black community at large wholly rejected a person's role assigned by white society, regardless of the person being enslaved or free. At Belvoir, Cinderella, despite being enslaved, married Brogden, a freed man. Although there was always the potential threat of Cinderella's sale and their potential children being enslaved, the commitment to each other persevered. The same marital arrangement and reality also applied to the Burley family, as well as countless other relationships facing these same oppressive pressures.

BUTTONS

When excavating African diaspora archaeology sites, we look for artifacts indicative of Africa, such as cowrie shells, colonoware (African-inspired pottery), or a spirit bundle related to the Bakongo religion. These cultural markers, however, are not always found on sites and do not necessarily move us closer to understanding the lived experiences of enslaved people. Some scholars suggest we instead seek out individual expressions of self by studying artifacts related to personal adornment (Singleton 1995:134; Wilkie 2000:10). One of the most prolific personal objects found on domestic archaeological sites is the button. Immediately upon digging inside and around the Belvoir Quarter, we found numerous buttons, many made from brass representing men's overcoats and waistcoats. We collected over 300 buttons from *inside* of the building with most found in the west side of the building and from the kitchen's subfloor pit (Figure 6.3).

Figure 6.3. Three shell buttons (*top row left*), two Prosser porcelain buttons (*top row right*), square black glass button (*second row far left*), two bone buttons (*second row middle and far right*), copper alloy shirt/dress buttons (*third row*), and copper alloy coat buttons (*bottom row*). (Courtesy of the Maryland Department of Transportation.)

We date historic buttons by studying the "shank" or loop on the back. The shank is diagnostic and can narrow down the manufacture date within a few decades, especially when cross-dating buttons with other artifacts on the site. The use of solder to attach the little piece of wire to the back as well as the shape of the loop shank is a diagnostic feature of copper alloy (brass) disc buttons. These disc buttons would have been sewn on coats, waistcoats, and breeches as both functional fasteners and perhaps, in some places, as decoration. In addition, women could have incorporated these buttons into their clothing as either a functional fastener or aesthetic piece. Out of the over 300 buttons recovered from Belvoir, 56 could be dated. Specifically, 71% of the flat brass buttons were manufactured before 1800, while the other 29% were produced after 1800. While some of the brass buttons were curated or lost during laundry activities, the high number of older buttons suggests the men enslaved by Scott dressed in formal attire more often than those enslaved by the Worthingtons or Welshes. In addition, these findings could also suggest these men may have consciously discarded the older buttons for new, shiny, and more stylish fasteners (Heath 1999).

To determine whether there was a type of garment button lost more often than others, I divided the 56 temporally diagnostic buttons by diameter. Those buttons under 18 mm in diameter likely attached to waistcoats, breeches, and sleeves. Regardless of the date, coat buttons appear to be the most frequently lost button type. Coat buttons are more numerous on the garment and can catch on furniture, doorways, or rub on items being carried. Also, coat buttons are more visible and may have been the ones to be replaced first. The other buttons we found within the home include 84 shirt, pants, and dress buttons made from bone, shell, Prosser porcelain, Goodyear hard rubber, and glass. Out of these buttons, bone (51%) was the most common. These organic fasteners belonged to both men's shirts and underwear. The next common button material other than metal was Prosser porcelain (33%), followed by shell (9%), Goodyear hard rubber (4 %), and black glass (3%). Beginning around 1840, Prosser porcelain buttons eventually replaced bone and shell buttons (Sprague 2002). It is likely most of the people enslaved by Thomas Welsh wore and lost the Prosser porcelain fasteners.

The high number of decorative buttons indicates clothes washing and mending within and around the stone quarter, but it also reflects choice and personalization of dress. Store ledgers and other historical accounts document the purchase of personal items by both free and enslaved people. Studies in Virginia, for example, revealed enslaved people purchased buttons, sleeve links, buckles, ribbons, and textiles from local stores (Heath 1999:52; Franklin 2019). This is important because it is possible for us to find, and hopefully recognize, individual choices and preferences by enslaved people in the archaeological record. Buttons sewn onto clothing could potentially reflect individual aesthetic choices as well as a person's status and knowledge of current fashion trends. The later 18th-century purchase and wearing of gold gilded over silver buttons by enslaved people, for example, may convey both awareness of fashion and the economic ability to stay up-to-date with the current trends (White 2005:51; Galle 2010:25,32). Galle (2010) suggests enslaved men's purchase and display of metal buttons on their chest during the 18th century was used as a "signaling" strategy within their community to communicate strength to resist assigned status and the ability to provide for family. Copper alloy buttons were expensive, so it may not have been possible to purchase multiple buttons or a set at a time. If the goal was to demonstrate awareness of current fashion, participation in the economy, and purchasing power, perhaps the display of stylish buttons, albeit mismatched, may have been sufficient.

In Southern Maryland, in consultation with the descendant community, we excavated a burial of an enslaved man interred between the 1780s and 1810s. He died in his 20s and was buried wearing pants and a waistcoat with mismatched buttons. Along the center of his body, we found five copper alloy and two tombac buttons (Cochran et al. 2016:166). Other archaeologists have observed assemblages where the buttons are similar in style but vary in the method of manufacturing. Although enslaved men likely preferred matching buttons, they may have obtained these fasteners one at a time, slowly adding to their vest or coat over time through purchase, trade, or as an incidental find (Smith 2017:228). While mismatched buttons should not be considered typical and may reflect limited resources and pure functionality, it urges us to consider the way enslaved men may have used these prosaic items to communicate awareness and economic freedom.

Finally, buttons may have also functioned to connect people and build relationships through button trading and gifting (Young 2004:144–146). There may have been specific designs on these flat disc fasteners associated with specific families, spiritual beliefs, or other unifying traits. At Belvoir we found U.S. Navy and U.S. Artillery military coat buttons dating to the first half of the 19th century. The variety of military buttons in the Belvoir Quarter suggests recycling of clothing and use of retired military uniforms, or it could communicate collecting behavior. If so, did the eagles or stars symbolize something other than the U.S. military to the person who wore them?

JEWELRY AND BEADS

Decorative personal artifacts beyond buttons include beads, delicate jewelry chains, and sleeve links worn at the neck, lower arm, or wrist. Newspaper ads and historical written accounts in the Chesapeake region mention enslaved women wearing earrings and sometimes rings on their fingers and jewelry around their necks (Heath 1999:56). These advertisements are very detailed, and scars are often mentioned, including on the ears from wearing jewelry. Near Millersville, about five miles from Belvoir, Margaret self-emancipated in 1852. The newspaper mentioned she had "two small lumps on the edge of her ears from piercing" (*BS* 1852b). Another similar ad stated Fanny had "holes prepared in her ears for rings" (*MG* 1805b). Men also wore jewelry. Jacob, who was manumitted on the Eastern Shore of Maryland in 1810, had holes in his ears for "bobbs"(Certificates of Freedom 1811). Store ledgers in Annapolis documented purchase of jewelry as well as ribbons, buttons, and ascots by enslaved people (Davidson Day Book 1774–1775). Inadvertently, these accounts captured their desire to express individuality by adorning their clothing, bodies, and hair with beads, jewelry, and ribbons. While we find personal artifacts in low numbers on archaeological sites, glass beads and bits of broken jewelry are common.

Men, women, and children wore beads as jewelry, wove them into hair, and sewed them onto clothing. These small round, oval, or faceted artifacts are flexible, allowing them to be displayed outwardly on oneself or secreted under clothing. Seen as a link to a collective cultural Africanism, or empowered and ready for ritual use and protection, blue beads are seen as culturally diagnostic (Shackel 2010:59). Some scholars have studied blue beads and wondered whether people of African descent viewed them as ritually powerful or are blue beads on African diaspora sites only coincidental (Thomas and Thomas 2004:113; Wheaton 1993:80). Furthermore, is our association of blue beads with ritual behavior from enslaved contexts dictated by actual patterns in the archaeological record? Is there evidence from Africa that links blue beads and the divine? As it turns out, both hold true.

In the Yoruba city of Ile-Ife, in southwestern Nigeria, archaeologists working on a historic period glass bead-manufacturing site found a significantly higher number of blue glass tube beads. In Yoruba culture, blue beads are significant and believed to be empowered with "ase," or vital force, and are considered medicine. As such, blue glass beads function to connect humans to the gods to "protect, heal and empower" themselves (Babatunde Babaloa et al. 2017:732–734). This is also true for many West and Central African cultures, many of whom use beads for self-adornment *and* rituals (Stine et al. 1996:54–55). If African cultures believed blue beads facilitated tapping into divine power, have we found evidence for this practice on North American enslaved domestic sites? Generally, we see a preference for blue beads by people of African descent in South Carolina and Georgia from the colonial through antebellum time periods (Stine et al. 1996:51–52). In comparison, the Chesapeake region, including Maryland, does not seem to see a strong representation of blue beads in African diaspora sites. Instead, red beads seem to dominate the collections (Agbe-Davies 2017:17). Of course, this could be a site sampling bias, a regional accessibility issue, or, perhaps more intriguing, a cultural preference by specific enslaved people. Although our current data cannot tease the details out of the blue bead phenomenon regarding regional distribution patterns and connection to specific African cultures, it would be a worthy pursuit.

Within and just outside of the Belvoir Quarter, we recovered fragments of broach pins, rings, and beads. We collected one dozen glass beads, four of which were seed beads (two red, one light blue, and one white). The larger beads included two blue multifaceted, barrel-shaped beads; three white wound beads; one colorless bead; one black round bead; and one round red, multifaceted bead (Figure 6.4). The numbers of beads on the site are not high enough or concentrated in any one area of the site to say anything concrete about behavior, but their presence is important. The people enslaved at Belvoir may have sewn these beads onto their clothing and hats, woven them into hair, hung them from the ears, or worn them around the wrist, ankle, or neck as jewelry. The round black bead found here may have even belonged to a rosary or been recycled from a broken one. We found most of the beads and all the seed beads in the kitchen's subfloor pit. Based on their context, and the presence of other beads outside of the building within a midden, these artifacts were likely inadvertently tossed away with other waste. Additionally, the seed beads were only found in this part of the site because the soils from the subfloor pits were water screened through a 1/8-inch sieve to capture small artifacts. As there was no evidence for these beads to be used in a ritual context, I instead consider how men, women, and children would have worn beads in their hair and around their neck and wrists. These rolled and pressed bits of glass could have provided them not only with a sense of power and protection but a feeling of uniqueness and self-expression. In addition to the traditional glass beads, we found pressed glass jewelry with two holes on each side. One was a colorless square glass bead with a pyramidal top while the other two were oval-shaped pressed black glass beads. It is possible they were once held in a setting and worn as a bracelet or other piece of jewelry.

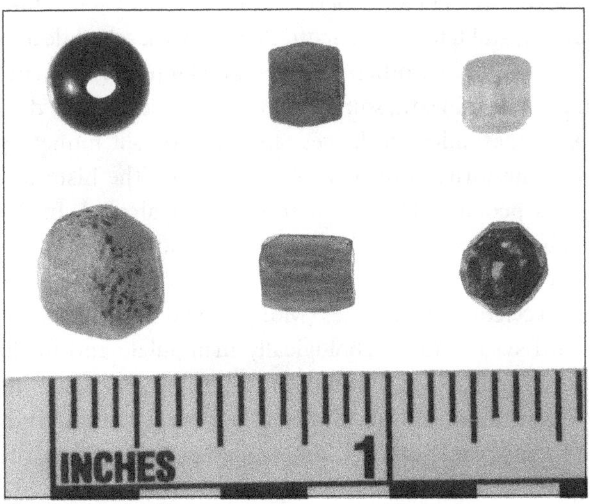

Figure 6.4. Round black glass bead, blue glass bead, and aqua glass bead (*top row*). Melted colorless bead, blue glass bead, and red glass bead (*bottom row*). (Courtesy of the Maryland Department of Transportation.)

We also collected two small copper alloy rings and a gold-plated wedding band. Rings during this period were worn on the fingers and on chains around the neck and sewn onto clothing. Women began wearing plain wedding bands by the early 19th century. Although the fourth finger traditionally receives the ring, some people wore rings on their thumb (White 2005:93). We also found a copper alloy crimped hoop earring. Hoop earrings were worn by both men and women but were primarily associated with the female gender by the late 18th century (White 2005:89–90). In this context, this jewelry speaks to the personal taste and expression of individuality and pride in self-adornment by the person who wore and lost this delicate earring. In addition to beads, jewelry, and waistcoat buttons, the Belvoir Quarter collection includes a parasol tip and purse hinges. These finds are not uncommon on wealthy estates. At the Hermitage, home of President Andrew Jackson, archaeologists recovered similar artifacts including cane tips, purse hinges, and parasol parts used by enslaved people (Thomas and Thomas 2004:120). These discoveries demonstrate their conscious and personal choice to incorporate accessories into their wardrobe and express economic status and independence to their community.

PERSONAL TIME

When reading through Clotworthy Birnie's (Scott's nephew) daily journal, I took note of the days he mentioned the enslaved workers' tasks. Each day, save Sunday, he documented the cutting of wood, the plowing of fields, or the washing of rye by Pompey and others. There were no entries for Sunday, Christmas day, or the day after Christmas. The planter considered these Christian days used by their enslaved people to attend church, pray, and remember the sabbath (Breeden 1980:258). To minimize downtime and maximize profits, Birnie modified work tasks if there was inclement weather. Taking instructions on planting and labor from Scott, Birnie's work schedule and treatment of enslaved people reflect other Chesapeake planters. At Christmas, the end of planting, or as a reward, some enslavers provided a large dinner, gifted alcoholic beverages, allowed dances, and/or gave out monetary bonuses for not resisting authority (Breeden 1980:276–279). The historical record mentions enslaved people drinking water as well as alcohol. In the last half of the 18th century, it would have been fairly common to serve rum or even cider to enslaved people as rewards for good behavior, during harvest time, for illness, or to celebrate Christmas (Morgan 1998:142). Enslavers regularly used the reward system to psychologically manipulate and instill compliance in the enslaved community through the following year. On Sundays, Belvoir's enslaved community would have visited family (if allowed) and traveled into town to trade and purchase food and other items. While the words from songs and conversations cannot be captured archaeologically, we do know they smoked tobacco from pipes, occasionally drank alcohol, and played jaw harps. The three jaw harps we found were broken and missing the tongue. Predating harmonicas, jaw harps would have been relatively inexpensive to purchase and easily carried in a pocket. They have been found on many sites including those in Virginia (Franklin 2019:139).

Figure 6.5. Marbles, doll parts, and a cast-iron toy wheel. (Courtesy of the Maryland Department of Transportation.)

We found evidence of children living, working, and playing in and around the stone quarter. The number of toys, however, is quite low for a home occupied for decades and suggests enslaved children entered the workforce quickly. We found three porcelain doll parts including a foot wearing a black painted heeled shoe, a leg fragment, and a hand from the home site. In addition, we collected a Frozen Charlie doll, the male version of a Frozen Charlotte, from a sandy layer of soil surrounding the northwest fireplace. Other toys include a ferrous, cast-iron wheel from a wheeled toy and a few clay marbles (Figure 6.5). While the porcelain dolls, for example, may have been played with by children, it is also possible they were used in West African spirit practices. In a cabin lived in by enslaved and freed African Americans in Montgomery County, Maryland, we found a porcelain doll's arm laid between stacked foundation stones (Schablitsky 2012:57). This discovery and the placement suggested participation in a protective ritual based on West African religious beliefs. I found the context of the Frozen Charlie at Belvoir curious; someone had incorporated it into a sandy layer with brick that formed the corner fireplace of the northwest bedroom. This feature was destroyed by 20th-century building construction, so it was impossible to confidently associate the porcelain doll with anything but the homeplace.

CLAY TOBACCO PIPES

Kaolin clay tobacco pipes are ubiquitous on historic period archaeological sites; we find them everywhere, including Belvoir. We collected and cataloged 721 kaolin clay tobacco pipe fragments from this site; 409 (57%) are bowls while 312 (43%) are stems. Tobacco smoking was likely enjoyed by enslaved men, women, and older children at Belvoir. Most of the decorated pipe bowls date to the first half of the 19th century. The most common pipe bowl style from the assemblage is ribbed, also referred to as cockled, around the pipe bowl. Some of the cockled bowl styles have ribbing reaching the rim of the bowl, while other designs stopped short. Some pipe bowls remained undecorated, while others displayed a "TD" stamped on the bowl, simple floral or leaf designs, and basket weave patterns. The initials "TD" are often associated with British pipe maker Thomas Dormer but, after 1780, may have just become a generic mark (Walker 2006). At least two different pipe bowls display a horse and another a bird (Figure 6.6).

Tobacco pipes could be given as gifts or rewards, but enslaved people also sought them out on their own, acquiring them through purchase, gifting, or trade. Smoking pipes can be highly stylized with different patterns; therefore, tobacco smokers often chose a design that resonated with them. When Africans first came to the Chesapeake region, they made their own pipes decorated with the Nigerian kwardata and cattle motif, symbols communicating status and identity (Emerson 1999:60–61). By the 18th century, the African design decorated tobacco pipe trade died out and was replaced with mass-produced white kaolin clay pipes from England. Although African artistic designed pipes were unavailable, tobacco pipes have always publicly displayed a person's identity in social settings. For the Irish, smoking a pipe stamped with a shamrock or "home rule" openly communicated resistance and their support for the Irish nationalist movement (Hartnett 2004:140–141). It is probable the pipe bowls held important personal symbolism for the enslaved people at Belvoir. We found two tobacco pipe bowls with a horse running with tail extended. During the 18th through 19th centuries, horse breeding and horse racing were enjoyed by many Chesapeake families, including Scott (Eareckson 1989). The men enslaved at Belvoir would

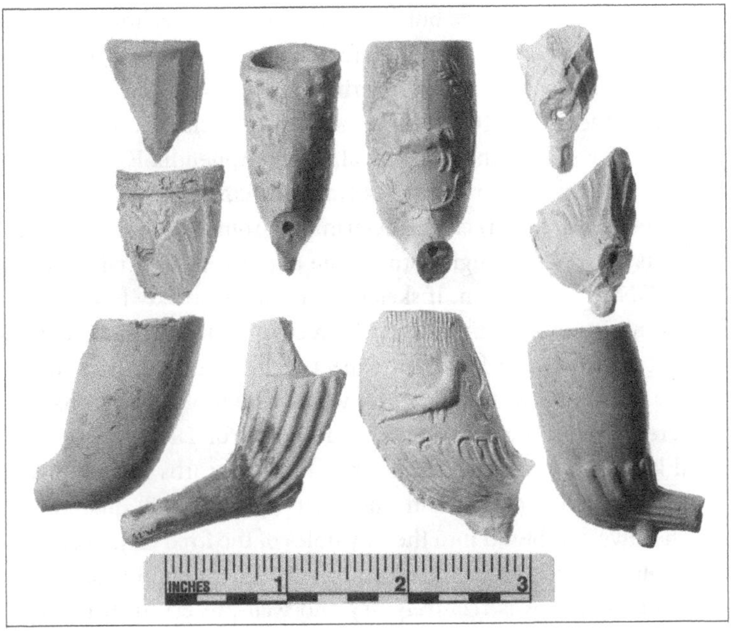

Figure 6.6. Clay tobacco pipe bowls with "TD," horse design, (*top row center*) and bird design (*bottom row, third from left*). (Courtesy of the Maryland Department of Transportation.)

have been responsible for the skilled care, training, and riding of horses (Mooney 2014). Perhaps these pipes were smoked by an enslaved man who rode or trained horses at Belvoir.

Another pipe bowl held the image of a bird. Its sleek body and angles of the feathers are suggestive of an eagle or hawk. Birds of prey are considered quite powerful with the BaKongo. A nkisi can be adorned with feathers from a bird of prey to empower it (MacGaffey 1990:55). Others studying African America affirm the belief that birds, particularly eagles, are seen as symbols of protection but also as warning signs (Gundaker 1998:66–68; Wilkie and Farnsworth 2005:279). While it is impossible to determine the meaning behind these designs, it is likely the images created feelings of familiarity and played into their decision on which pipe to press to their lips and hold in their hand.

DNA FROM TOBACCO PIPESTEMS

The archaeology and tax record confirm the Belvoir Quarter was a home for enslaved people. But was there a way to prove people of African descent lived there? Could we find genetic material in the form of DNA buried in this house? Archaeologists have been attempting to recover human DNA from artifacts for the last 20 years, but it is not a common technique because of the high cost of analysis and high risk for negative results (Schablitsky 2006). In Maryland, we had difficulty recovering intact DNA from human skeletal remains buried less than 100 years because of the acidic and high moisture content of clayey soils (Schablitsky et al. 2019b:Appendix E). In most cases, the DNA is too degraded and only sex (male or female) and general ancestry (e.g., African vs. European) can be determined from the human bone. Forensic scientists and archaeologists know site context and burial environment are key to DNA preservation. If skeletal material is quickly buried and fluctuations in moisture are minimized, the recovery of DNA increases (Leney 2006; Surat 2018). While I did not expect to discover human bones under the Belvoir Quarter, it was probable we would find broken clay tobacco pipestems there. Pipestems are the perfect candidate for DNA testing since the low-fired kaolin clay is very porous and readily absorbs moisture. When a person places a tobacco pipestem into their mouth, it will quickly wick up DNA-rich saliva and blood into the tiny holes of the fired clay. Since much of the archaeological site lay protected under subsequent buildings, the flooring inside of the quarter was relatively dry and well-preserved. If the soils and artifacts were protected from weather and moisture, these conditions would increase the chance of recovering human DNA from clay pipestems.

In anticipation of submitting tobacco pipestems to an ancient DNA laboratory, I created a collection kit with sterile forceps, paper envelopes, and acid-free plastic bags. As expected, we found numerous pipestems inside and outside of the home in our screens and nestled between brick flooring. When a pipestem was found, I personally collected the artifact without anyone else contaminating the sample. Although it can be possible to detect modern DNA contamination from historic period DNA, using a single archaeologist to collect samples ensures consistency of method and reduces additional contamination. From within and outside of the stone quarter, I collected four pipestems and placed them in a freezer. Once out of the field, the four pipestems were sent to Ripan Malhi and Kelsey Witt at the University of Illinois Urbana–Champaign. Here, they attempted to extract DNA from the four artifacts. Malhi and Witt successfully recovered degraded DNA from two of the four pipestems. They learned women smoked the pipes and one of the pipestems, PS96, held enough genetic material to assess the pipe smoker's ancestry. They transferred the data to Hannes Schroeder at University of Copenhagen who compared the degraded genetic material against a database of modern Africans. He determined this broken clay tobacco pipe, PS96, was smoked by a woman who was most genetically similar to the Mende of Sierra Leone, West Africa (Schablitsky et al. 2019a). Although we were able to recover the sex and ancestry of this person, the DNA was too badly degraded to link to living descendants. This was still an exciting discovery since we now have the potential to identify the ancestry of people who left personal artifacts behind on an archaeological site. In this case, we were able to connect a specific group of people in Africa to a historic estate in Maryland.

The close study of these small items found at Belvoir confirms what we know about the lives of enslaved people. First, they had the ability, opportunity, and access to participate in the selling, trading, and buying of animals, dishware, and personal items. While the enslaver provided food provisions and household items, it should not overshadow their own resourcefulness and production of food and crafts for sale or trade in exchange for plates, cups, and personal items. Second, enslaved people used clothing fasteners and decorative jewelry to communicate community and individual preferences and behaviors. Archaeological sites often hold broken porcelain bric-a-brac, for example, that can speak to a household's expendable income and someone's conscious effort to personalize a room, perhaps even to communicate affection for a particular figure or animal. In this homeplace, we only recovered a few toys and objects to personalize the space. While we did not find significant evidence of decorating the interior of the home, the enslaved household did wear beads and jewelry to display their individual style. Perhaps the focus on self-adornment rather than space decoration is a statement of how the enslaved people physically and mentally separated themselves from their situation. The stone, brick, and mortar of the quarter communicated functional living and working space rather than a home of their own. Furthermore, Scott did not construct the quarter as a place to nurture individuality, preference, or social status for those who entered the home.

The analysis of the buttons along with the distribution of clothing buckles reflects a decline in the estate owner's wealth and the ability of the enslaved people to secure and access personal items. Under Scott, the enslaved men living in the stone quarter wore coats, waistcoats, and pants closed at the knee with brass fasteners while the enslaved household associated with the Worthington and Welsh families wore clothing consistent with manual labor fastened with bone and Prosser porcelain buttons.

Although in limited number, we recovered items associated with music and tobacco smoking. The enslaved community played jaw harps, smoked tobacco from clay pipes, and occasionally drank alcohol. Tobacco pipe smoking was significant within and around the stone quarter. The most interesting discovery from the site was the DNA lifted from a pipestem. With scientific certainty, we know a woman linked to the Mende people of Sierra Leone, West Africa, lived at Belvoir. This is exciting for Maryland but also for potentially unlocking additional data about the movement of people and African cultures across the eastern United States.

7

Resisting and Concluding

Truth crushed to earth shall rise again.

—William Cullen Bryant (1840:269)

Almost everything that stands above ground and buried below Belvoir was touched, formed, and shaped by enslaved people. The archaeological site, cleared land, terraced gardens, and the remaining manor home are the physical evidence of their labor and their lives. While pulling the artifacts out of the ground and touching the foot-worn bricks, I tried to imagine what these enslaved Marylanders looked like and tried to comprehend their daily challenges. A button leads to curiosity about the clothing they wore, and then about a person's life. How did others view them, and how did they see themselves? If enslaved, did they think about self-liberating, and what was their interaction like with the enslaver? Their thoughts are impossible to know, and these types of questions have no simple or single answer. What is certain, however, is the enslavers' intentions regarding enslaved people were self-serving. They kept human property for agricultural and household labor in a manner that facilitated sexual and physical abuse. There were no altruistic acts or attempts at unconditional relationships between them, the wicked system did not allow it. While levels of cruelty against enslaved people by enslavers and overseers fluctuated, the perceived and actual threat of violence was consistent (Farnsworth 2000). The enslaved community lived in an environment of perpetual anxiety and fear of being punished, separated from family, starved, raped, or killed. The things Belvoir's enslaved people left behind tell us this.

RESISTANCE

At Belvoir there were active episodes of resistance ranging from self-emancipation to taking food. In between, there was controlled chaos outwardly appearing as compliance and production. This estate was always a contested landscape. The enslavers exercised paternalistic authority over their buildings, animals, wives, children, and human chattel. They aspired to be viewed as socially and physically superior by their peers. Historic documents hint at white society's perception of Belvoir's esteemed planter families, remembering them as local celebrities descended from royalty. John Ross was remembered at his death as an "indulgent master"(*MG* 1766). His identity was strongly connected to power and control over enslaved Africans and the wealth they brought him and his family. The obituary attempted to humanize Ross by insinuating he was generous and overly kind to his human chattel. In truth, these men were greedy and their existence during a certain time in history does not excuse their participation in human trafficking and abuse. Scott, in his letters to his nephew Birnie, appears conflicted about slave labor. On one hand, he simply needed workers at a reasonable cost, but there was a labor shortage, and he concluded there was no other choice but to use enslaved people. His issue with slavery was not a moral conflict but an economic one. Furthermore, Scott encouraged Birnie to form familial bonds with his enslaved people to make them stay put, malleable, and loyal. When a married couple self-emancipated from Birnie, Scott discouraged him from splitting the pair up through a sale. Out of impulsive frustration, Birnie sold them anyway. Scott likely saw his nephew compromising one form of psychological control of enslaved people for another. Enslavers reduced elopement and resistance through either encouraging the formation of families and positive rewards or through physical abuse, intimidation, and/or the threat of sale beyond state lines. Scott may have seen encouraging the formation of families as less dramatic and more effective than violence, hence the discouraging words to Birnie.

The Worthingtons behaved similarly to Birnie; punishment included iron collars and chains for those who resisted and selling young married women, like Cinderella, beyond Maryland to maximize profit and solve chronic resistance. Affluent Annapolitans ostracized George Worthington for threatening to sell Cinderella to pay off his debts, but it is hard to tell whose side they were on. While their ultimate goal was to free Brogden from the state penitentiary, they were quick to distinguish their altruistic intensions from those of the delusional abolitionists.

While everyone responded to entrapment differently, most enslaved people likely resisted in some form and at some time in their lives, but finding evidence in the archaeological record is difficult. Rebelling against their situation was often measured and subtle and took the form of occasional acts such as a broken tool, working slowly, or providing misinformation (Orser 1989:35–36; Orser and Funari 2001:62–63). While those enslaved at Belvoir surely participated in similar acts, I wondered whether their defiance was inadvertently recorded in the artifacts within the home, and could we decipher them? Could we detect their anxiety about and fear of an enslaver or overseer in the archaeological record, and what would that look like? Indeed, people turn to religion to quell feelings of powerlessness and to ask assistance from the spiritual realm. Not surprisingly, we occasionally find evidence of enslaved households turning to religion to help protect them. We did not, however, identify evidence of spirit practices or minkisi in this archaeological site. Instead, the enslaved people may have considered alternative ways to protect themselves against physical threats and bodily harm.

We found a number of artifacts associated with control, protection, hunting, and food processing around the Belvoir Quarter. Indeed, the presence of knives and gun-related artifacts in enslaved contexts can be interpreted in multiple ways. As mentioned, we found lead shot, a flint wrap, and gunflints. It does not, however, mean that the enslaved people owned the guns or were allowed to keep the weapons in the quarter. Our archaeological work did not find gun parts. Additionally, the lead shot likely came from shot animals, and the gunflints may have been repurposed for strike-a-lights to create sparks for fires. On occasion, the enslaved people may have borrowed a firearm from their enslaver to hunt or to euthanize a suffering animal; however, it is unlikely they kept a gun for an extended period. Only in rare cases did enslaved people successfully negotiate to keep a firearm at their side or in their home (Morgan 1998:389–390). While keeping a gun within arm's length would have been convenient for hunting, enslaved people also recognized a firearm as a solution to minimize the risk of violence against them and their family from an overseer, enslaver, or others in the community (Odewale 2016:164, 270). Knives and sharp tools could also be seen as protection against an oppressor. The Belvoir Quarter excavations revealed 18 knives with 7 (39%) associated with the subfloor pit. Only two of these could be considered table knives while the others were more substantial or used as tools including a chamfer and drawknife. In addition, the enslaved household had a metal file, ax fragment, and a bayonet in this hand-dug cellar. The bayonet, dating to the time of the American Revolution, was found on top of the kitchen's subfloor pit. It may have been collected from Rochambeau's encampment and carried to the quarter to be repurposed as a tool or saved for protection. Local scavenging of the abandoned camp may be another reason we never found Rochambeau's site.

The relatively high number of tools and knives in this household feature suggests a few different scenarios. While some of the knives could have been broken during use in the kitchen and then tossed away, it is difficult to explain the presence of broken outdoor tools such as a file, ax, and chamfer/drawknives. Perhaps an enslaved laborer broke the tool, and, to avoid working or being reprimanded for the damage, they hid them. It is also possible that the broken tools may have been an opportunistic find, and, instead of being tossed away, the knife could be repurposed and used as their own. Keeping a sharp instrument, "just in case," surely provided some measure of comfort.

While the tools and knives held in the subfloor pit had the potential to be retrieved and brandished as a weapon to protect themselves or used for a benign purpose, Belvoir's enslaved households were more likely using prosaic material culture daily to foster individuality, strengthen community, and resist. It is difficult to find signs of African culture or resistance in an artifact assemblage (Orser and Funari 2001). Sometimes evidence of agency can be in hand, but the way we "see" the artifact through our own cultural lens causes misinterpretations. Anthropomorphic images and art fired onto dishware and molded onto pipe bowls held symbolism for some enslaved people who continued to practice their religion. The creation of a nkisi is an example where the material and color of objects rather than the function was significant to people engaging in West African spirt practices. As Theresa Singleton (1995) teaches us, we must stop seeing enslaved people interacting with their physical and social environment like a European enslaver; teacups can be scoops for spicy stews and enslaved status can be meaningless within their community. This paradigm shift allows us to interpret archaeology of the African diaspora more accurately. Most importantly, enslaved people are seen as active participants rather than passive and reactionary characters in their lives.

There are also artifacts that suggest discrete behaviors took place within the Belvoir Quarter. We collected 10 slate pencils or styluses and several slate tablet fragments from the site. We did not find them inside the home, only outside and mixed in with other household debris from the first half of the 19th century. In any other context, I would connect the broken slate and lost styluses with school-aged children actively learning arithmetic and writing. Here, writing artifacts say and mean something different. Enslavers discouraged enslaved people from reading and writing to limit their knowledge, resourcefulness, and independence. Within the quarter, slate boards and pencils may have been used to supplement the memory of the cook, allowing her to facilitate the tallying of supplies and recalling recipes. In this context, she may have negotiated the possession and use of writing supplies to scratch a line or create lists. Perhaps during times of independence and resistance they taught themselves and each other how to read and write with these slate artifacts. Writing skills facilitated enslaved people's ability to communicate both casual information and clandestine plans. These skills could be used to fabricate manumission papers allowing enslaved people to pass for free and reach

Pennsylvania. Cinderella's sister, Eliza, was able "to read and write well" when she self-emancipated from George Worthington's home in Washington, D.C. Worthington suspected Eliza may have forged papers, protecting her from detainment (*BS* 1852a).

CONCLUSION

During this archaeological project, we were fortunate enough to connect with the biological descendants of the Burley and the Brogden families; however, there are countless other descendants driving along General's Highway past Belvoir who are unaware of their connection to this place. Some of them may not be interested in Maryland history or the genealogy of their family. Others may find their connection to enslaved ancestors too painful and traumatic to even confront. Those biological descendants who do want to connect with their past and learn about their heritage approach the opportunity with gratitude and humility. They appreciate the suffering and sacrifices their many great-grandparents made so they could have their life. Some descendants feel a responsibility to remember, record, and pass down their family history to the next generation. They advocate and ask us to incorporate archaeology and history into the public school system to ensure each child hears these stories in a way that makes them feel proud to be descended from a strong and determined people.

What the archaeological study of Belvoir has taught us is to approach an archaeological site with a difficult history by asking and answering two important questions before we begin: Who is this history for, and how can it benefit the living? As a white archaeologist digging into the traumatic history of Black people, I am aware of my limitations and biases and appreciate the importance of ensuring the entire archaeology team is respectful and sensitive during the scientific process of recovery and discovery. While this is U.S. history and Maryland's past, it is most importantly the descendant community's heritage. My collective experiences with Belvoir's descendants, the relatives of the Donner Party of California (where some emigrants resorted to cannibalism to survive), and Harriet Tubman's family have shown me how strongly and personally descendant communities connect to their ancestors and the historic landscape. Within many of these descendants is a feeling of responsibility to physically visit the discovery site with their families, particularly their children. It is important for youth to absorb the experience in a manner that instills pride and recognition of the strength and perseverance of their ancestors. While we shudder at the system of slavery, and the horrible conditions enslaved people were forced to endure, a family member's perspective is different. When reflecting, they simultaneously feel a range of emotions ranging from elation to sadness. There is a spiritual appreciation and a physical pain for the ancestors' sacrifices so they and their children could be born. Descendants stand on an archaeology site knowing this truth, hoping grandmother and grandfather are proud of them, wondering whether they have done enough good in their lives to justify their suffering. As archaeologists, we need to ask ourselves a similar question. Are we doing enough to ensure descendent communities can access their heritage? There are always new and creative ways to engage with our public, and there must be sincere relationships with those whose history we are studying. Their questions should be folded into our research agenda, and they must always be consulted throughout the process. Opportunities to share new history, artifacts, and experiences should be incorporated into accessible media including school curricula, publications, and personal engagement with the archaeology site through hands-on experiences. Only through deliberate and consistent inclusion of descendant families' questions and concerns will a project yield its potential. Just as importantly, an archaeological site linked to the African diaspora should always serve as a therapeutic space for reflecting and remembering (Figure 7.1).

Figure 7.1. Descendants standing within the footprint of the Belvoir Quarter. *Left to right*, Nancy Daniels, Sheila Brogden-Jefferson, Wanda Watts, Larry Brogden, Pamela Brogden, Shelley Evans, and Erica Jones. (Courtesy of the Maryland Department of Transportation.)

Epilogue

THERE WAS ONE last question Belvoir's descendants and visitors always asked us: Where were the enslaved people buried? Usually, the planter allowed a small area of land, sometimes overlooking a ravine or body of water, to be used to bury their dead. Often, the patch of land could not be farmed; perhaps it was too rocky or just a flat knoll. Their burying ground was never too close or too far away to carry a loved one to their final resting place. In contrast, the Ross, Key, and Maynadier families buried their dead to the south of the manor home, on a road toward Annapolis. Their family cemetery survives in the adjacent subdivision, marked with upright stones, protected by a fence, and preserved by the homeowner's association under a carpet of vinca. While the burying ground for Belvoir's enslaved community was lost to us, it was remembered by others.

After we closed the archaeology site, I received a call from Rodney Daff, who grew up at Belvoir in the 1970s and early 1980s. He heard about the archaeological discovery and wanted to share something with us. During their childhood, Daff and his cousin James "Jamie" Brown Jr. had been shown the location of a "slave cemetery." Within two weeks of the call, we met on site in front of the flattened mound where the Belvoir Quarter once stood. Daff and Brown excitedly took the lead down the old road that wound behind the archaeology site. I followed them through the woods and arrived on a flat landing perched over a steep ravine. It was a prominent parcel, just a short walk from the quarter, yet private enough to retain a sense of serenity. Brown pointed to a rectangular tabular piece of white marble, next to a west–east facing depression. A vandal had broken the marker in two. Despite angling the stone in the sunlight, we could not read any name or date. The inscription eroded away years ago. Pushing leaves back with our feet, we began to find "fieldstones," individually placed grave markers taken from the bedrock eroding out of the knoll. Along the edge were snagged cedar trees. Although we did not have rows of formal headstones with people's names and dates of birth and death, the presence of the white marble, a depression likely associated with a sunken grave, a dozen fieldstones, and cedar trees suggested a historic burial ground. I contacted the Burley and Brogden descendants and told them we may have found their ancestors' burying ground.

We did not want to disturb the human burials through excavation, and, as ground-penetrating radar was not immediately possible due to thick vegetation, we used human remains detection dogs to confirm the cemetery. Dogs have been used for over 20 years to locate buried human remains that are hundreds of years old (Baxter and Hargrave 2015:60–90; Glavas and Pintar 2018). Canines possess the ability to locate various strengths of human decomposition odor across a variety of settings. In fact, human remains possess a different chemical signature than other mammals and include 478 different volatile organic compounds (Vass et al. 2008; Glavas and Pintar 2018: 1107). Through rigorous training, dog handlers teach canines how to distinguish from other dead mammals and "alert" on human remains, including those buried in the ground. The canines signal the presence of cadaver decomposition islands or scent pools by giving their human handler a signal such as lying down or pawing the ground. The best time to use human remains detection dogs to search for human burials is usually in the morning when it is cool and moist. Sometimes, the canines benefit from probing the ground to release the odor trapped in the soil.

Heather Roche often works for law enforcement finding modern human remains. She also trains her canines on historic cemeteries to detect subtle and historic scent evidence from human decomposition. Raven, a senior Belgian Malinois, and a young black Labrador named Partner arrived at the site with the descendant community. First on scene was Partner who ran up the hill and immediately stopped in his tracks, hitting an invisible scent wall. His nose down, he worked the ground back and forth, alerting to the scent of human decomposition by laying down on multiple spots. Roche put Partner away, and Raven went to work; she also alerted. Roche and her canines successfully confirmed what Daff and Brown knew: this was a burying ground, and it likely held the people enslaved at Belvoir.

Watching on the side were the descendants. Shelley Evans became tearful; she was amazed and wondered whether her ancestors were buried there. Pamela Brogden thought of Cinderella, remembering how she tried to get away, passing away soon after being caught (*Washington Post* 2018). The discovery of the burial ground was an important final step in the descendants' archaeological journey to find their family. There are no further plans to excavate or delineate the graves.

References Cited

Agbe-Davies, Anna S.

2017 Where Tradition and Pragmatism Meet: African Diaspora Archaeology at the Crossroads. *Historical Archaeology* 51(1):9–27.

Annapolis Gazette

1864 Negro Soldiers. March 3.

Anne Arundel County Manumission Record

1803 Jeremiah Tanner Manumission Record. 1797–1851. CM48–1, vol. 825, p. 153. Maryland State Archives, Annapolis.

Anne Arundel County Marriage Licenses

1825 Anne Arundel County marriage license record. November 22. Maryland State Archives, Annapolis.

Anne Arundel County Pardon Record.

1851 Secretary of State (Pardon Record) Abraham Brogden. May 23. F. 121, MdHR 7931, S 1108–2. Maryland State Archives, Annapolis.

Anne Arundel County Slave Statistics

1864 Anne Arundel County Commissioner of Slave Statistics. 01/03/10/040/ MdHR 4748, C142–1. Maryland State Archives, Annapolis.

Babatunde Babalola, Abidemi, Susan Keech McIntosh, Laure Dussubieux, and Thilo Rehren

2017 Ile-Ife and Igbo Olokun in the History of Glass in West Africa. *Antiquity* 91(357):732–750.

Ball, Charles

1859 *Fifty Years in Chains: The Life of an American Slave*. H. Dayton Publisher, Indianapolis, Indiana.

Baltimore Sun (BS)

1848 Runaway Advertisement for Cinderella Placed by Edward H. Brown, Overseer for Geo. F. Worthington. December 23.

1852a Runaway Advertisement for Eliza Brogden Placed by G. F. Worthington. February 11.

1852b Runaway Advertisement for Margaret Rogers Placed by Dr. Wm. Sands. August 10.

Barton, Christopher P.

2022 *The Archaeology of Race and Class at Timbuctoo: A Black Community in New Jersey*. University Press of Florida, Gainesville.

Battle-Baptiste, Whitney

2007 "In This Here Place": Interpreting Enslaved Homeplaces. In *Archaeology of Atlantic Africa and the African Diaspora*, edited by Akinwumi Ogundiran and Toyin Falola. Indiana University Press, Indiana.

2010 Sweepin' Spirits: Power and Transformation on the Plantation Landscape. In *Archaeology and Preservation of Gendered Landscapes*, edited by Sherene Baugher and Suzanne M. Spencer-Wood, pp. 81–94. Springer, New York.

Baumgarten, Linda

1988 Clothes for the People, Slave Clothing in Early Virginia. *Journal of Early Southern Decorative Arts* 14(2):26–70.

Baxter, Carey L., and Michael L. Hargrave

2015 Guidance on the Use of Historic Human Remains Detection Dogs for Locating Unmarked Cemeteries. U.S. Army Corps of Engineers, Engineer Research and Development Center.

Belvoir Camp

1781 Belvoir Camp description. Untitled manuscript. HM 621 U8 B3. Huntington Library, San Marino, California.

Blankespoor, Juliet

2018 Violet's Herbal and Medicinal Uses. Chestnut School of Herbal Medicine (website). Updated June 8, 2023, accessed July 1, 2024.

Bloch, Lindsay, and Anna S. Agbe-Davies

2017 "With Sundry Other Sorts of Small Ware Too Tedious to Mention," Petty Consumerism on U.S. Plantations. In *Material Worlds, Archaeology, Consumption, and the Road to Modernity*, edited by Barbara J. Heath, Eleanor E. Breen, and Lori A. Lee, pp. 119–140. Routledge, London.

Bowes, Jessica, and Heather Trigg

2012 Social Dimensions of Eighteenth- and Nineteenth-Century Slaves' Uses of Plants at Poplar Forest. In *Jefferson's Poplar Forest: Unearthing a Virginia Estate*, edited by Barbara J. Heath and Jack Gary, pp. 105–128. University Press of Florida, Gainesville.

Breeden, James O. (editor)

1980 *Advice among Masters, the Ideal in Slave Management in the Old South*. Greenwood Press, Westport, Connecticut.

Breslaw, Elaine G.

1975 Wit, Whimsy, and Politics: The Uses of Satire by the Tuesday Club of Annapolis, 1744 to 1756. *William and Mary Quarterly* 32(2):295–306.

Brooks, Alasdair M.

1997 Beyond the Fringe: Transfer-Printed Ceramics and the Internationalization of Celtic Myth. *International Journal of Historical Archaeology* 1(1):39–55.

Brophy, Juliet K., and Kevin Crisman

2013 A Taphonomic Evaluation of Three Intact Pork Barrels from the Steamboat "Heroine" (1838). *Historical Archaeology* 47(4):71–85.

Bryant, William Cullen

1840 The Battlefield. In *Poems*. Harper and Brothers, New York.

Burley Manumission

1854 Anne Arundel County, Manumission Record, 1844–1866. Volume 832, p. 86, March 3, 1854. Maryland State Archives, Annapolis.

Cochran, Mathew, Matthew Palus, and Julie M. Schablitsky

2016 Archaeological Survey and Corridor Study along MD 231, Benedict, Charles County, Maryland. Vol. 1. Maryland State Highway Administration, Baltimore.

Callcott, Margaret Law (editor)

1991 *Mistress of Riversdale: The Estate Letters of Rosalie Stier Calvert, 1795–1821.* Johns Hopkins University Press, Baltimore, Maryland.

Certificates of Freedom

1811 Manumission of Jacob by Peter Harrington. Dorchester County Court, 1806–1851. Maryland State Archives, Annapolis. C689–1.

Condon, John Joseph, Jr.

2001 Manumission, Slavery and Family in the Post-Revolutionary Rural Chesapeake: Anne Arundel County, Maryland, 1781–1831. Ph.D. dissertation, University of Minnesota, Minneapolis.

Crader, Diana C.

1990 Slave Diet at Monticello. *American Antiquity* 55(4):690–717.

Crowl, Heather, Peter Regan, and Benjamin Stewart

2022 Archaeological Investigations of Scott's Estate (Belvoir), Anne Arundel County, Maryland. Maryland State Highway Administration Archaeological Report No. 480, Baltimore. On file at the Maryland Historical Trust, Crownsville.

Daily National Intelligencer

1823 January 28. Washington, D.C.

Davidson Day Book

1774–1775 John Davidson Day Book, Annapolis Merchant, December 3, 1774–August 23, 1775. MS 281, Maryland Historical Society, Baltimore, Maryland.

Davidson, James M.

2021 The Subfloor-Pit Tradition in the United States: A Florida Case Study and Critical Reappraisal of Its Origins. *Historical Archaeology* 55(3): 353–377.

2023 Padlocks as Negotiated Freedoms within Enslavement. *International Journal of Historical Archaeology* 27:898–952.

Dornan, Jennifer L.

2002 Agency and Archaeology: Past, Present and Future Directions. *Journal of Archaeological Method and Theory* 9(4):303–329.

Douglass, Frederick

1845 Narrative of the Life of Frederick Douglass. Anti-Slavery Office, Boston, Massachusetts.

Eareckson, Jean Lee

1989 Dr. Upton Scott. SC 4071-1-17. Maryland State Archives, Annapolis.

Edgar, Lady Matilda Ridout

1912 *A Colonial Governor in Maryland: Horatio Sharpe and His Times, 1753–1773*. Longmans, Green, London.

Ellis, Clifton

2010 Building for "Our Family, Black and White," the Changing Form of the Slave House in Antebellum Virginia. In Ellis and Ginsburg, *Cabin, Quarter, Estate*, pp. 141–155.

Ellis, Clifton, and Rebecca Ginsburg

2010 *Cabin, Quarter, Estate. Architecture and Landscapes of North American Slavery*, edited by Clifton Ellis and Rebecca Ginsburg. Yale University Press, New Haven, Connecticut.

Emerson, Matthew C.

1999 African Inspirations in a New World Art and Artifact: Decorated Tobacco Pipes from the Chesapeake. In *"I, Too, Am America" Archaeological Studies of African-American Life*, edited by Theresa A. Singleton, pp. 47–75. University Press of Virginia, Charlottesville.

English, A. J.

1990 Salted Meats from the Wreck of the "William Salthouse": Archaeological Analysis of Nineteenth Century Butchering Patterns. *Australian Journal of Historical Archaeology* 8:63–69.

Farnsworth, Paul

2000 Brutality or Benevolence in Plantation Archaeology. *International Journal of Historical Archaeology* 4(2):145–158.

Federal Tax Assessment

1783 Upton Scott, Providence, pt, 626 acres. Anne Arundel County, Severn Hundred, p. 3. S 1161-1-13. Maryland State Archives, Annapolis.

1798 Henry Maynadier, 893 acres, Anne Arundel County, Severn Hundred and South River Hundred. 1798 Federal Direct Tax, vol. 729, p. 287. Maryland State Archives, Annapolis.

Federal Writers' Project (FWP)

1941 *Slave Narratives, a Folk History of Slavery in the United States from Interviews with Former Slaves*, Vol. 8, *Maryland Narratives, The Federal Writers' Project, 1936–1938*, Library of Congress, Washington, D.C.

Fennell, Christopher C.

2011 Early African America: Archaeological Studies of Significance and Diversity. *Journal of Archaeological Research* 19(1):1–49.

Fesler, Garrett

2004 Living Arrangements among Enslaved Women and Men at an Early Eighteenth-Century Virginia Quartering Site. In *Engendering African-American Archaeology: A Southern Perspective*, edited by Jillian E. Galle and Amy L. Young, pp. 177–236. University of Tennessee Press, Knoxville.

2010 Excavating the Spaces and Interpreting the Places of Enslaved Africans and Their Descendants. In Ellis and Ginsburg, *Cabin, Quarter, Estate*, pp. 27–49.

Foner, Philip S. (editor)

1999 *Frederick Douglass: Selected Speeches and Writings*. Lawrence Hill, Chicago.

Franklin, Maria

2001 The Archaeological Dimensions of Soul Food: Interpretating Race, Culture and Afro-Virginian Identity. In *Race and the Archaeology of Identity*, edited by Charles Orser, pp. 88–107. University of Utah Press, Salt Lake City.

2004 An Archaeological Study of the Rich Neck Slave Quarter and Enslaved Domestic Life. Colonial Williamsburg Research Publications, Colonial Williamsburg Foundation, Virginia.

2015 Diaspora Foodways. In *The Archaeology of Food: An Encyclopedia*, edited by Karen Metheny and Mary Beaudry, pp. 133–135. Rowman and Littlefield, Lanham, Maryland.

2019 Enslaved Household Variability and Estate Life and Labor in Colonial Virginia. *International Journal of Historical Archaeology* 24:115–155.

Galle, Jillian E.

2010 Costly Signaling and Gendered Social Strategies among Slaves in the Eighteenth-Century Chesapeake: An Archaeological Perspective. *American Antiquity* 75(1):19–43.

Gallo, John

1985 *Nineteenth and Twentieth Century Yellow Ware*. Heritage Press, Richfield Springs, New York.

Glavas, Vedrana, and Andrea Pintar

2018 Human Remains Detection Dogs as a New Prospecting Method in Archaeology. *Journal of Archaeological Method and Theory* 26(3):1106–1124.

Greer, Georgeanna H.

1981 *American Stonewares: The Art & Craft of Utilitarian Potters*. Schiffer Books, Atglen, Pennsylvania.

Greer, Matthew C.

2020 Making Time for Tea(wares): Slow Archaeology, Enslaved Life, and the Poetics of Consumption. Paper presented at the 53rd Annual Meeting of the Society for Historical Archaeology, Boston, Massachusetts.

Guilland, Harold F.

1971 *Early American Folk Pottery*. Chilton Book, Philadelphia, Pennsylvania.

Gundaker, Grey

1998 *Signs of Diaspora/Diaspora of Signs*. Oxford University Press, New York.

Hammond, John Martin

1914 *Colonial Mansions of Maryland and Delaware*. J. P. Lippincott, Philadelphia, Pennsylvania

Handler, Jerome, and Diane Wallman

2014 Production Activities in the Household Economies of Plantation Slaves: Barbados and Martinique. *International Journal of Historical Archaeology* 18(3):441–466.

Hartnett, Alexandra

2004 The Politics of the Pipe: Clay Pipes and Tobacco Consumption in Galway, Ireland. *International Journal of Historical Archaeology* 8(2):133–147.

Haskin, Leslie A.

1941 *Pioneer Stories of Linn County, Oregon*. Vol. 1. WPA Interviews. Early Pioneer Publications, Albany, Oregon.

Heath, Barbara J.

1999 Buttons, Beads, and Buckles: Contextualizing Adornment within the Bounds of Slavery. In *Historical Archaeology, Identify Formation, and the Interpretation of Ethnicity*, edited by Maria Franklin and Garrett Fesler, pp. 47–69. Colonial Williamsburg Foundation Library, Williamsburg, Virginia.

2004 Engendering Choice: Slavery and Consumerism in Central Virginia. In *Engendering African American Archaeology: A Southern Perspective*, edited by Jillian E. Galle and Amy L. Young, pp. 19–38. University of Tennessee Press, Knoxville.

Heath, Barbara J., and Amber Bennett

2000 "The Little Spots Allow'd Them": The Archaeological Study of African-American Yard. *Historical Archaeology* 34(2):38–55.

Henson, Josiah

1849 *Life of Josiah Henson, Formerly a Slave, Now an Inhabitant of Canada*. Entered by Arthur D. Phelps. Bolles and Houghton, Cambridge, Massachusetts.

Hooks, Bell

2015 *Yearning. Race, Gender, and Cultural Politics*. Routledge, New York.

Howard Papers

1662–1919 John Eager Howard Papers. Box 19, MS 469. Maryland Historical Society, Baltimore, Maryland.

Hughes, George W.

1845 Economical Dwellings for Estate Labor. In *The Cultivator*. Vol. 2. Albany, New York.

Hunter, Robert, and Marshall Goodman

2005 The Destruction of the Benjamin DuVal Stoneware Manufactory, Richmond, Virginia. In *Ceramics of America*, edited by Robert Hunter, 37–60. Chipstone Foundation. University Press of New England, Hanover, New Hampshire.

Johnson, Nathaniel, Enid Schildkrout, Donna Gherlerter, Dana Elmquist, and Dale Rosengarten

2008 *Grass Roots: African Origins of an American Art*. Teacher's Guide. Museum for African Art, New York.

Johnston, Allan

1987 Being Free: Black Migration and the Civil War. *Australasian Journal of American Studies* 6(1):3–21.

Katz-Hyman, Martha B., and Kym S. Rice

2010 *World of a Slave: Encyclopedia of the Material Life of Slaves in the United States*. Greenwood Press, Santa Barbara, California.

Keim, Alexander

2020 Stories from the Kitchen: Analysis of Ceramics Recovered from the Belvoir Slave Quarters. Paper presented at the 53rd Annual Meeting of the Society for Historical Archaeology, Boston, Massachusetts.

Kelso, William M.

1984 *Kingsmill Estates, 1619–1800: Archaeology of Country Life in Colonial Virginia.* Academic Press, Orlando, Florida.

Key, Francis Scott

1819 Francis Scott Key to Henry Maynadier, letter, November 26, 1819. Gilder Lehrman Collection, GLC02379, online access.

Kimmel, Richard H.

1993 Notes on the Cultural Origins and Functions of Sub-Floor Pits. *Historical Archaeology* 27(3):102–113.

Kollmann, Dana

2016 Bioarchaeological Examination of Human Remains Recovered from the Serenity Farm Burial Ground (18CH839), Benedict, Charles County, Maryland, Appendix A. In Cochran et al., Archaeological Survey and Corridor Study along MD 231, Benedict, Charles County, Maryland.

Kryder-Reid, Elizabeth

1998 The Archaeology of Vision in Eighteenth-Century Chesapeake Gardens. In *Annapolis Pasts: Historical Archaeology*, edited by Paul A. Shackel, Mark S. Warner, and Paul R. Mullins, pp. 268–290. University of Tennessee Press, Knoxville.

Larson, Kate Clifford

2004 *Harriet Tubman, Portrait of an American Hero: Bound for the Promised Land.* Random House, New York.

Leibowitz, Joan

1985 Yellow Ware; the Transitional Ceramic. Schiffer Publishing, Exton, Pennsylvania.

Leney, Mark

2006 Sampling Skeletal Remains for Ancient DNA (aDNA): A Measure of Success. *Historical Archaeology* 40(3):31–49.

Leone, Mark P.

1988 The Relationship between Archaeological Data and the Documentary Record: Eighteenth Century Gardens in Annapolis, Maryland. *Historical Archaeology* 22(1):29–35.

2005 *The Archaeology of Liberty in an American Capital: Excavations in Annapolis.* University of California Press, Berkeley.

Leone, Mark P., and Paul A. Shackel

1990 Plane and Solid Geometry in Colonial Gardens in Annapolis, Maryland. In *Earth Patterns: Essays in Landscape Archaeology*, edited by William M. Kelso and Rachel Most, pp. 153–169. University Press of Virginia, Charlottesville.

Letzer, Mark B., and Jean B. Russo (editors)

2003 *The Diary of William Farris: The Daily Life of an Annapolis Silversmith.* Maryland

Historical Society, Baltimore.

Lev-Tov, Justin S. E.

1998 Zooarchaeology and Social Relations in Annapolis, Maryland. In *Annapolis Pasts: Historical Archaeology in Annapolis, Maryland*, edited by Paul A. Shackel, Paul R. Mullins, and Mark S. Warner, pp. 119–146. University of Tennessee Press, Knoxville.

Levine, Ellen

2007 *Henry's Freedom Box: A True Story from the Underground Railroad.* Scholastic, New York.

Levine, Peter

1981 Draft Evasion in the North during the Civil War, 1863–1865. *Journal of American History* 67(4): 816–834.

Levinthal, Aaron

2020 The Unique Architecture of the Quarters for the Enslaved at Belvoir. Paper presented at the 53rd Annual Meeting of the Society for Historical Archaeology, Boston, Massachusetts.

Lovit, Alex

2011 "The Bounds of Habitation": The Geography of the American Colonization Society, 1816–1860. Ph.D. dissertation, Department of History, University of Michigan, Ann Arbor.

Lucas, Michael T.

2014 Empowered Objects: Material Expressions of Spiritual Beliefs in the Colonial Chesapeake Region. *Historical Archaeology* 48(3):106–124.

MacGaffey, Wyatt

1990 The Personhood of Ritual Objects: Kongo Minkisi. *Etnofoor* 3(1):4–61.

Maryland Gazette (MG)

1756 Dr. Upton Scott and Elizabeth Ross Marriage Announcement. September 9.

1766 John Ross Obituary. September 25.

1790 Runaway Advertisement for Charles Placed by Brice T. B. Worthington. January 10.

1805a Runaway Advertisement for Henny Placed by John L. Dickinson. September 5.

1805b Runaway Advertisement for Fanny placed by Henry Johnson. April 4.

1815 Anne Arundel County Justices of the Peace Appointments by Governor . March 2.

1816 Belvoir for Sale. February 29.

1823 Runaway Advertisement for Basil Placed by Thomas Welsh. January 30.

Maryland Inventory of Historic Properties

1983 Griffith-Worthington House. Annapolis, Anne Arundel County, Maryland.

Maryland Journal (MJ)

1780a Runaway Advertisement, January 11.

1780b Runaway Advertisement, June 6.

1790 Runaway Advertisement, January 15.

Matchett's Baltimore City Directory

1853–1854 Vol. 564:26. Maryland State Archives, Annapolis.

Maynadier, Henry

1812 Henry Maynadier to Clotworthy Birnie, letter, November 23. SC 5818-1-1. Maryland State Archives, Annapolis.

1814 Henry Maynadier to Clotworthy Birnie, letter, March 26. SC 5818-1-1. Maryland State Archives, Annapolis.

McKee, Larry

1999 Food Supply and Estate Social Order: An Archaeological Perspective. In *"I, Too, Am America" Archaeological Studies of African-American Life*, edited by Theresa A. Singleton, pp. 218–239. University Press of Virginia, Charlottesville.

Mooney, Katherine C.

2014 *Race Horse Men: How Slavery and Freedom Were Made at the Racetrack*. Harvard University Press, Cambridge, Massachusetts.

Morgan, Philip D.

1998 *Slave Counterpoint: Black Culture in the Eighteenth-Century Chesapeake and Lowcountry*. University of North Carolina Press, Chapel Hill.

Mullins, Paul R.

1999 *Race and Affluence: An Archaeology of African America and Consumer Culture*. Kluwer Academic, New York.

Neiman, Frasier D.

2008 The Lost World of Monticello: An Evolutionary Perspective. *Journal of Anthropological Research* 64(2): 161–193.

Niemcewicz, Julian Ursyn

1965 *Under Their Vine and Fig Tree: Travels through America in 1797–1799, 1805, with Some Further Account of Life in New Jersey*. Translated and edited by Metchie J. E. Budka. Collections of the New Jersey Historical Society. Vol. 14. Grassmann Publishing, Elizabeth, New Jersey.

Odewale, Alicia

2016 Living among Presidents and Kings: Enslaved Africans Coping with Risk in Service to the Elite. Ph.D. dissertation, Department of Anthropology, University of Tulsa, Oklahoma.

Orser, Charles E., Jr.

1989 On Plantations and Patterns. *Historical Archaeology* 23(2):28–40.

Orser, Charles E., Jr., and Pedro P. A. Funari

2001 Archaeology and Slave Resistance and Rebellion. *World Archaeology* 33(1):61–72.

Perdue, Charles L., Thomas E. Barden, and Robert K. Philips

1976 *Weevils in the Wheat: Interviews with Virginia Ex-Slaves*. University of Virginia Press, Charlottesville.

Pogue, Dennis J.

2002 The Domestic Architecture of Slavery at George Washington's Mount Vernon. *Winterthur Portfolio* 37(1):3–22. University of Chicago Press.

2023 Documenting the Domestic Architecture of Chesapeake Slavery. Historic St. Mary's City Lecture Series, St. Mary's City, Maryland.

Provincial Court Land Records

1758 Provincial Court Land Records, 1756–1759. Vol. 702, pp. 334–336. Maryland State Archives, Annapolis.

Reitz, Elizabeth J.

1987 Vertebrate Fauna and Socioeconomic Status. In *Consumer Choice in Historical Archaeology*, edited by Suzanne Spencer Wood, pp. 101–119. Plenum Press, New York.

Risse, Guenter B.

1992 Medicine in the Age of Enlightenment. In *Medicine in Society: Historical Essays*, edited by A. Wear, pp. 149–196. Cambridge University Press, Cambridge.

Ross, John

1766 John Ross Last Will and Testament. Huntington Collection, Wills Liber C.G. no. 1, vol. 33, 1764–1766, TE1–7. Maryland State Archives, Annapolis.

Samford, Patricia

2007 *Subfloor Pits and the Archaeology of Slavery in Colonial Virginia*. University of Alabama Press, Tuscaloosa.

Sanford, Douglas W.

2022 Slave Houses in the 1860 U.S. Census for the State of Maryland. A Comparison with Slave-Related Buildings on File with the Maryland Historical Trust. Maryland Historical Trust, Crownsville.

Sanford, Douglas W., and Dennis J. Pogue

2009 *Vernacular Architecture Newsletter* 122 (Winter 2009):1, 3–8.

Savitt, Todd L.

2002 *Medicine Slavery: The Diseases and Health Care of Blacks in Antebellum Virginia*. University of Illinois Press, Champaign.

Schablitsky, Julie M.

2006 Genetic Archaeology: The Recovery and Interpretation of Nuclear DNA from a Nineteenth Century Hypodermic Syringe. In Remains of the Day: Forensic Application in Archaeology, edited by Julie M. Schablitsky. *Historical Archaeology* 40(3):8–19.

2007 A Redware Jar on Every Table: The Archaeology of the Simmons House and Boston Town, Thompson Mills State Heritage Site, Lin County, Oregon. University of Oregon, Museum of Natural and Cultural History and State Museum of Anthropology. Report 2007–003. Eugene, Oregon.

2012 Meanings and Motivations Behind West African Spirit Practices. In Historical Archaeology and the Importance of Material Things, Vol. 2, edited by Julie M. Schablitsky and Mark P. Leone, pp. 45- 63. *Historical Archaeology*, Special Publication Series 9.

Schablitsky, Julie, Karen Hutchins-Keim, Aaron Levinthal, and Jason Shellenhamer

2019b Archaeology and History of the Simon Hill Cemetery, Hyattsville, Prince George's County, Maryland. Maryland Department of Transportation, State Highway Administration, Baltimore.

Schablitsky, Julie M., Kelsey E. Witt, Jazmin Ramos Madrigal, Martin R. Ellegard, Ripan S. Malhi, and Hannes Schroeder

2019a Ancient DNA Analysis of a Nineteenth Century Tobacco Pipe from a Maryland Slave Quarter. *Archaeological Science*, May, 11–18.

Scott, Elizabeth M.

2001 Food and Social Relations at Nina Plantation. *American Anthropologist* 103(3):671–691.

Scott, Upton

1764 Upton Scott to Francis Scott, letter, January 2. SC 4071–1-1. Maryland State Archives, Annapolis.

1806 Upton Scott to Clotworthy Birnie, letter, October 16. SC 4071, 2–5. Maryland State Archives, Annapolis.

1812a Upton Scott to Clotworthy Birnie, letter, March 8. SC 4071 2–6. Maryland State Archives, Annapolis.

1812b Upton Scott to Clotworthy Birnie, letter, January 18. SC 4071 2–6. Maryland State Archives, Annapolis.

1812c Upton Scott to Clotworthy Birnie, letter, June. SC 4071–2-6–10. Maryland State Archives, Annapolis.

Selig, Robert A.

2015 Historical Research Report on Belvoir ("Scott's Estate") from the Earliest Known Date of European Contact to the Present with a Particular Focus on the Encampment of French Forces on the Site on 17/18 1781. Prepared for URS Corporation under contract to Maryland Department of Transportation, State Highway Administration, Baltimore.

Seligman, Samuel K., Thomas W. Cuddy, Amelia G. Chisholm, Kristofer M. Beadenkopf, Matthew Palus, and Mark P. Leone

2006 Final Report of the Phase III Archaeological Investigations at the Dr. Upton Scott House (18AP18). Annapolis, Anne Arundel County, Maryland, 1998–1999.

Shackel, Paul A.

2010 Identity and Collective Action in a Multiracial Community. *Historical Archaeology* 44(1):58–71.

Singleton, Theresa A.

1995 The Archaeology of Slavery in North America. *Annual Review of Anthropology* 24:119–140.

Smith, F. S. Key

1909 A Sketch of Francis Scott Key, with a Glimpse of His Ancestors. *Records of the Columbia Historical Society*, Washington, D.C., 12: 71–88.

Smith, Johanna Hope

2017 Adorned Identities: An Archaeological Perspective on Race and Self-Presentation in Eighteenth-Century Virginia. Ph.D. dissertation, University of Tennessee, Knoxville.

Sprague, Roderick

2002 China or Prosser Button Identification and Dating. *Historical Archaeology* 36:111–127.

Stearns, Samuel

1801 *The American Herbal, or, Materia Medica*. Walpole, Massachusetts.

Stine, Linda France, Melanie A. Cabak, and Mark D. Groover

1996 Blue Beads as African-American Cultural Symbols. *Historical Archaeology* 30(3):49–75.

Surat, P.

2018 Overcoming DNA Degradation in Forensic Science. *News-Medical* (website), accessed July 1, 2024.

Thomas, Brian W.

1998 Power and Community: The Archaeology of Slavery at the Hermitage Estate. *American Antiquity* 63(4):531–551.

Thomas, Brian W., and Larissa Thomas

2004 Gender and the Presentation of Self: An Example from the Hermitage. In *Engendering African American Archaeology*, edited by Jillian E. Galle and Amy L. Young, pp. 101–131. University of Tennessee Press, Knoxville.

Thompson, Robert Farris

1983 *Flash of the Spirit: African and Afro-American Art and Philosophy*. New York: Vintage Books.

1990 Kongo Influences on African-American Artistic Culture. In *Africanisms in American Culture*, edited by Joseph E. Holloway, pp. 148–184. Indiana University Press, Bloomington.

1993 *Face of the Gods: Art and Altars and Altars of Africa and the African Americas*. Prestel, Munich, Germany.

Upton, Dell

2010 White and Black Landscapes in Eighteenth-Century Virginia. In Ellis and Ginsburg, *Cabin, Quarter, Estate*, pp. 121–139.

U.S. Civil War Draft Record

1863 Thomas Welsh. U.S. Civil War Draft Registrations Records, 1863–1865. Records of the Provost Marshal General's Bureau (Civil War), Record Group 110. National Archives, Washington D.C.

U.S. Civil War Pension Index

1861–1934 U.S. Civil War Pension Index: General Index to Pension Files, 1861–1934. Filed in 1924 for Nathan Brisco. National Archives and Records Administration, Washington, D.C.

U.S. Federal Agricultural Census

1850 Agricultural and Manufacturing Census Records, Anne Arundel County. SM 61–150. Maryland State Archives, Annapolis.

1860 Agricultural and Manufacturing Census Records, Anne Arundel County. SM 61–22. Maryland State Archives, Annapolis.

U.S. Federal Census

1830 Population Schedules of the Fifth Census of the United States, Anne Arundel County, Annapolis, Maryland. National Archives and Records Administration, Washington, D.C.

1840 Population Schedules of the Sixth Census of the United States, Anne Arundel County, Annapolis, Maryland. National Archives and Records Administration, Washington, D.C.

1860 Population Schedules of the Eighth Census of the United States, Anne Arundel County, Annapolis, Maryland. National Archives and Records Administration, Washington, D.C.

1870 Population Schedules of the Ninth Census of the United States, Philadelphia, Pennsylvania. National Archives and Records Administration, Washington, D.C.

1880 Population Schedules of the Tenth Census of the United States, Philadelphia, Pennsylvania. National Archives and Records Administration, Washington, D.C.

1910 Population Schedules of the Thirteenth Census of the United States, Philadelphia, Pennsylvania. National Archives and Records Administration, Washington, D.C.

U.S. Naval Enlistment Record

1870 U.S. Naval Records, 1855–1891. Weekly return of enlistments at Naval Rendezvous ("Enlistment Rendezvous"), January 6, 1855–August 8, 1891. M1953, Roll 39, 2383639. National Archives, Washington, D.C.

Vass, Arpad. A., Rob R. Smith, Cyril V. Thompson, Michael N. Burnett, Nishan Dulgerian, and Brian A. Eckenrode

2008 Odor Analysis of Decomposing Buried Human Remains. *Journal of Forensic Science* 53(2):384–391.

Vlach, John Michael

1993 *Back of the Big House, The Architecture of Estate Slavery.* University of North Carolina Press, Chapel Hill.

WBAL-11

2020 Interview. Baltimore, Maryland, February 25.

Walker, Iain C.

2006 An Archaeological Study of Clay Pipes from the King's Bastion, Fortress of Louisbourg, Canadian Historic Sites. *Occasional Papers in Archaeology and History* 2.

Walsh, Lorena S., Ann Smart Martin, and Joanne Bowen

1997 Provisioning Early American Towns: The Chesapeake: A Multidisciplinary Case Study. Manuscript, Colonial Williamsburg Foundation, National Endowment for the Humanities Grant RO-22643–93.

Warden, David Bailie

1811 Journal of a Voyage from Annapolis to Cherbourg. On Board of the Frigate Constitution, Aug. 1 to Sept. 6. Reprinted June 1916 in *Maryland Historical Magazine* 11(2):127–141.

Warfield, Joshua Dorsey

1905 *The Founders of Anne Arundel and Howard Counties, Maryland: A Genealogical and Biographical Review from Wills, Deeds and Church Records.* Kohn & Pollock, Baltimore, Maryland.

Washington, Booker T.

1901 *Up from Slavery: An Autobiography.* Doubleday, Garden City, New York.

Washington Post

2018 Cedar Trees and Fieldstones: A Likely Slave Cemetery Is Unearthed near Annapolis. March 9.

Wetherill, Susan R.

1989 Belvoir Title Search Narrative. On file, Maryland Department of Transportation, State Highway Administration, Baltimore.

Wheaton, Thomas R.

1993 Archaeological Testing of Willow Hall and Walnut Grove Estates. Report prepared by New South Associates, Stone Mountain, Georgia. Submitted to USDA Forest Service, Francis Marion National Forest, Columbia, South Carolina.

White, Carolyn L.

2005 *American Artifacts of Personal Adornment, 1680–1820, A Guide to Identification and Interpretation.* AltaMira Press, Lanham, Maryland.

Wilkie, Laurie A.

1996 Medicinal Teas and Patent Medicines: African-American Women's Consumer Choices and Ethnomedical Traditions at a Louisiana Plantation. *Southeastern Archaeology* 15(2):119–131.

2000 Culture Bought: Evidence of Creolization in the Consumer Goods of an Enslaved Bahamian Family. *Historical Archaeology* 34(3):10–26.

Wilkie, Laurie A., and Paul Farnsworth

1999 Trade and the Construction of Bahamian Identity: A Multiscaler Exploration. *International Journal of Historical Archaeology* 3(4):283–320.

2005 *Sampling Many Pots: An Archaeology of Memory and Tradition at a Bahamian Plantation.* University Press of Florida, Gainesville.

2010 Those Who Were Traded: African-Bahamian Archaeology and the Slave Trade. In *Social Archaeologies of Trade and Exchange: Exploring Relationships among People, Places, and Things*, edited by Alexander A. Bauer and Anna S. Agbe-Davies, pp. 143–163. Left Coast Press, Walnut Creek, California.

Williams, Susan

1996 *Savory Suppers and Fashionable Feasts: Dining in Victorian America.* University of Tennessee Press, Knoxville.

Wilson, Kristin J., and Melanie A. Cabak

2004 Feminine Voices from Beyond the Grave: What Burials Can Tell Us about Gender Differences among Historic African Americans. In *Engendering African American Archaeology: A Southern Perspective*, edited by Jillian E. Galle and Amy L. Young, pp. 263–285. University of Tennessee Press, Knoxville.

Worthington, Brice John

1837 Last Will and Testament. Maryland State Archives, Annapolis.

Worthington, George F.

1871 *Sacred Poems*. Published by the author, Baltimore, Maryland.

1875 Light Shining out of Darkness by a Blind Clergyman. Published by the author, Baltimore, Maryland.

Worthington, Noah

1852–1856 Noah Worthington Home Remedies. MS 924, Box 3. Maryland Historical Society, Baltimore.

Worthington, Thomas Carroll, Jr.

2015 Worthington Family History Interview, conducted by Julie Schablitsky, November 15, 2015. On file at Maryland Department of Transportation, State Highway Administration, Baltimore.

Yentsch, Anne E.

1994 *A Chesapeake Family and Their Slaves: A Study in Historical Archaeology*. Cambridge University Press, Cambridge.

Young, Amy L.

2004 Risk and Women's Roles in the Slave Family: Data from Oxmoor and Locust Grove Estates in Kentucky. In *Engendering African American Archaeology: A Southern Perspective*, edited by Jillian E. Galle and Amy L. Young, pp. 133–150. University of Tennessee Press, Knoxville.

Index